Editors
Kathy Humrichouse
Sara Connolly

Editorial Project Manager
Betsy Morris, Ph.D.

Editor in Chief
Sharon Coan, M.S. Ed.

Creative Director
Elayne Roberts

Production Manager
Phil Garcia

Imaging
Alfred Lau

Acknowledgements
Trademarks: Trademarked names and graphics appear throughout this book. Instead of listing every firm and entity which owns the trademarks or inserting a trademark symbol with each mention of a trademarked name, the publisher avers that it is using the names and graphics only for editorial purposes and to the benefit of the trademarked owner with no intention of infringing upon that trademark.

Publishers
Rachelle Cracchiolo, M.S. Ed.
Mary Dupuy Smith, M.S. Ed.

Computer Projects
for
Middle Schools

Author

Steve Butz

Teacher Created Materials, Inc.
6421 Industry Way
Westminster, CA 92683
www.teachercreated.com
ISBN-1-57690-709-1
©2000 Teacher Created Materials, Inc.
Made in U.S.A.

Table of Contents

Table of Contents *(cont.)*

Computer Projects for Middle Schools: An Introduction

Computer Projects for Middle Schools is designed to introduce students of all ability levels to the fundamental operation of a personal computer, while at the same time providing them with the knowledge of how computer technology is applied in our society. This book was created for use in a computer lab setting for grades six through eight, and each lesson can easily be correlated to the existing middle-school curriculum.

The twelve activities contained in this book address the many different ways computers can be used. This offers teachers the opportunity to confidently take their classes to the computer lab and present well-rounded lessons.

This book is arranged in a logical progression that includes introductory labs, intermediate labs, and advanced labs. Everything you need to implement each lesson effectively is contained within the lab, along with helpful template files that provide you with any required resource material.

Each activity has been successfully used in the middle school classroom. Each can be completed in one or two forty-five minute computer lab sessions. Little knowledge of computers is required to teach the activities contained in this book. Each lab provides you with the overall purpose of the lesson, learning objectives, materials required, and step-by-step procedures detailing how to successfully implement the lesson.

Computer Projects for Middle Schools can be used in either a Macintosh or Windows platform. Every lesson explains how to execute the lab in either platform, using a variety of software. This book should be especially appealing to teachers of middle school technology, who are implementing new information technology lessons into their existing curriculum. Each lab in this book can be used to teach information technology, as well as aligning the technology curriculum with the other middle school disciplines.

As you work through each lab, this chart will assist you in following the directions for the activity.

Instruction	What To Do
BOLD CAPITALS	Select this pulldown menu from the Menu Bar.
Bold Italics	Make this selection from the pulldown menu.
Bold	Choose this button, tool, or key.
(*filename*)	Type this word or sentence, or this is the name of a file.

Overall, *Computer Projects for Middle Schools* is an easy to use, fun, and educational way to provide your students with computer literacy, while keeping your computer lab time productive and in line with your curriculum.

How to Use the CD-ROM

The Read Me File found on the CD-ROM provides a list of file names and indicates whether a file is an example, template, or graphic.

The CD-ROM included in this kit contains resource files for the activities. The CD-ROM does not contain the software applications indicated in the labs for this book. The applications (e.g., *AppleWorks*, *Microsoft Office*, etc.) must be installed on your computer system prior to using the resource CD-ROM.

Labs #1 and 2 have example files on the CD-ROM. You can use these to check student progress, or to see for yourself how the finished activity should look.

Labs #4, 5, 7, 10, 11, and 12 have template files that your students can use for the labs in the interest of saving time. For example—Lab #4 focuses on using a spreadsheet with human population growth data to create a line chart. The first six steps contain instructions for setting up the spreadsheet. But maybe your students are spreadsheet experts, and you feel that it would be a waste of time for them to create the spreadsheets themselves. The template provides the completed spreadsheet. Students can simply open the template from the CD-ROM and create a line chart of the data provided. The first page of each lab indicates at which step to begin if you choose to use the template.

The template files have been saved in the formats indicated in the labs. Whenever possible, the files have been saved so that they can be opened by many versions of each program. For example— *AppleWorks* (*ClarisWorks*) files have been saved in *ClarisWorks* 4.0 format, *Microsoft Excel* files have been saved in *Microsoft Excel* 5.0/95 format, etc.

Template files are meant to be opened and immediately saved under another name somewhere on your desktop, hard drive, or floppy diskette. That way the original template file is always intact and ready to use again and again. So, if you open a template file, before entering any text or data, click on the **File** menu and select **Save As**. Navigate to where you want to save the file, rename it, and then click on the **Save** button. Then you can begin entering text and data, knowing that the original file is still intact. That's all there is to using a template file!

You might wish to create a folder on your desktop or hard drive and download all the template files from the CD-ROM into it. Then you can direct your students to access this folder whenever they are completing an activity that requires a template.

Also included on the CD-ROM are two graphic files that students will import into their drawing documents in Labs #6 and 9. Directions for importing these files are included in the labs.

Lab #1 Introduction to Spreadsheets: The Multiplication Table

Purpose:

Students are introduced to the basic formatting of cells in a spreadsheet application by creating their own multiplication tables.

Learning Objectives:

At the end of this lesson, each student will be able to:

- create a new spreadsheet document.

- utilize the **Select All** command.

- define the terms: *column*, *row*, and *cell*.

- identify the specific address of a selected cell.

- adjust the width of a selected column.

- adjust the height of a selected row.

- enter data into a specific cell.

- increase the size of the font in a selected cell.

- alter the color of the font in a selected cell.

- change the style of the font in a specific cell

- adjust the alignment of the data in a specific cell.

- create a heading for a spreadsheet.

- create an accurate multiplication table using a spreadsheet application.

Materials:

- *AppleWorks* (*ClarisWorks*), *Microsoft Excel* for Macintosh or Windows, or another spreadsheet application

Lab #1 *(cont.)*

Procedure:

1. To begin this activity, explain to your students that they are going to use a spreadsheet application to create a multiplication table. Ask them if they have ever used a spreadsheet before. Explain to the class that a spreadsheet is like a word processing application for numbers. Spreadsheets are used to organize and manipulate specific data. Data entered into a spreadsheet can be in the form of either numbers or text, and spreadsheets are most often used to display information in the form of charts or graphs.

2. After you have discussed the basics of how spreadsheets are used, instruct your class to open new spreadsheet documents. Take a minute to explain the basic structure of a spreadsheet. First, point out that the spreadsheet is like a big grid pattern that is made up of columns and rows. Columns make up the vertical part of the spreadsheet and are labeled with letters. Rows compose the horizontal portion of the spreadsheet and are labeled with numbers. Together, columns and rows compose an entire spreadsheet, and where a column meets a row is called a cell. Spreadsheets contain thousands of cells, and each cell has its own location or address. For example, cell A1 is located where row 1 meets column A. This method of cell identification allows the spreadsheet to perform mathematical calculations.

3. Next, instruct your class to locate column A on their spreadsheets. Explain to them that the width of a column can be altered to fit the data entered into a cell. To change the size of a single column, students should bring their cursors up to the top of column A. They then move their cursors to the line located between columns A and B, and the shape of the cursor should change. (See Figure 1.)

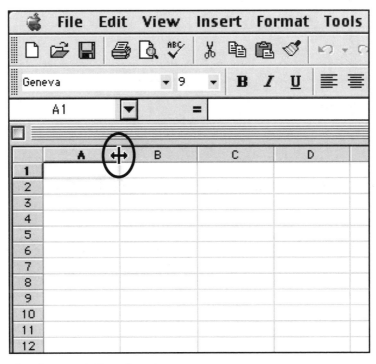

Figure 1. Adjustment of column width using the mouse

Lab #1 *(cont.)*

4. Once your students have their cursors in the correct location, the shape should change to a line with two arrows pointing outward. Your students should now hold down the mouse button and drag to the right. The width of column A increases. Clicking and dragging the mouse to the left decreases the column width.

5. Once your class has mastered this task, inform them that it is also possible to increase the width of all of the columns in the entire spreadsheet at the same time. This is accomplished by going to the **EDIT** menu and choosing the *Select All* command. The entire spreadsheet should now be highlighted. Students should place their cursors in between any of the column labels, then click and drag to alter the width of all of the columns in the spreadsheet.

6. Now instruct your class that they can also alter the height of a row the same way they altered the width of a column. Students should bring their cursors over to the row labels and move them over the line in between each row until the cursor changes shape. Then they should click and hold the mouse button, moving it either upward to increase the row height, or downward to decrease the row height. (See Figure 2.)

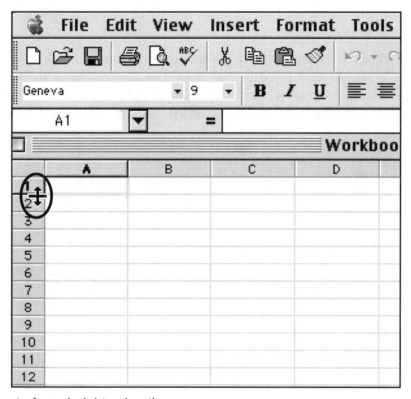

Figure 2. Adjustment of row height using the mouse

Lab #1 *(cont.)*

7. Once your class has become comfortable with altering the size of rows and columns, they can begin to construct their multiplication tables. Have students first select cell B1, which is the address of the cell where column B intersects row 1. Have them notice that the cell address is also shown in the upper left part of the screen. Next they should enter the number (*1*) into cell B1, and then press the **Tab** key on their keyboards. Ask them what happened. They should respond that their cursors moved to cell C1. In this cell they should enter the number (*2*) and then press the **Tab** key again. They should continue to enter numbers until they reach cell K1, which should contain the number (*10*).

8. After they have filled in row 1, they should click into cell A2 and enter the number (*1*) into this cell. Next, they should press **Return** or **Enter** on their keyboards. This will take them down to cell A3. They should then continue to fill the cells in column A with numbers up to (*10*), which should be in cell A11. The resulting spreadsheet should resemble the one in Figure 3.

	A	B	C	D	E	F	G	H	I	J	K
1		1	2	3	4	5	6	7	8	9	10
2	1										
3	2										
4	3										
5	4										
6	5										
7	6										
8	7										
9	8										
10	9										
11	10										

Figure 3. Cells correctly filled with numbers

9. Now that your students' multiplication table spreadsheets are beginning to take shape, have them go to the **EDIT** menu on the Menu Bar and choose *Select All*. This will highlight all of their cells. Next, they should increase the size of their font to 18 point. This is accomplished in *AppleWorks* (*ClarisWorks*) by choosing the **FORMAT** menu, selecting *Size*, and choosing **18-point**. In *Microsoft Excel*, students can increase the font size by clicking the **Font Size** window and selecting size **18**. The numbers in their cells should now be too large to fit. This can be fixed by keeping the entire spreadsheet highlighted while adjusting the column width and row height in order to make the cells large enough. Instruct your class to adjust their cell sizes using the Select All technique, allowing their numbers to fit perfectly in each cell.

Lab #1 *(cont.)*

10. After they have completed this task, they should align the numbers to the center of each cell. To accomplish this in *AppleWorks (ClarisWorks)*, students should keep the spreadsheet highlighted, select the **FORMAT** menu, and choose *Alignment*, then *Center*. In *Microsoft Excel*, they can align the cell data to the center by clicking the **Align Center** button on their toolbar. Once this is accomplished, their spreadsheets should resemble the one in Figure 4.

	A	B	C	D	E	F	G	H	I	J	K
1		1	2	3	4	5	6	7	8	9	10
2	1										
3	2										
4	3										
5	4										
6	5										
7	6										
8	7										
9	8										
10	9										
11	10										

Figure 4. Cells re-sized with data aligned to the center

11. Instruct your students to highlight only the cells in row 1 that contain data. This is accomplished by clicking cell A1, holding down the mouse button, and dragging to cell K1. If they are using *AppleWorks (ClarisWorks)*, students should then open the **FORMAT** menu and choose *Shadow* to change the style of the numbers in the selected cells. They should repeat this task for the cells in column A. In *Microsoft Excel*, instruct your class to choose the **FORMAT** menu, and select *Cells*. Here they should choose the **Font** tab from the dialog box and check the **Shadow** box. After they have altered the style of their font, they should choose the **EDIT** menu, and then *Select All*. Now instruct your class to change the color of the font for their multiplication tables. In *AppleWorks (ClarisWorks)*, selecting the **FORMAT** menu and choosing *Text Color* changes the color of the font. In *Microsoft Excel*, change the color by once again selecting the **FORMAT** menu, choosing *Cells*, and clicking the **Font** tab from the dialog box. Suggest to the class that they select a dark-colored font so that they can easily see the numbers.

Lab #1 *(cont.)*

12. The last task your class should perform to complete the formatting of the multiplication table is to insert a header. If they are using *Microsoft Excel* to construct their multiplication tables, they should insert a header by choosing ***Page Setup*** from the **FILE** menu and selecting the **Header/Footer** tab from the dialog box. In *AppleWorks* (*ClarisWorks*) a heading is inserted by selecting the **FORMAT** menu and choosing ***Insert Header***. Instruct your class to insert the header (*Multiplication Table*) along with their first and last names.

13. Now that their multiplication tables have been formatted, instruct your class to fill in the correct numbers. To do this, they must first multiply the numbers in row 1 by the numbers in column A. They enter the product in the cell where the row and column meet. Their completed multiplication spreadsheets should resemble the one in Figure 5. When they have completed their spreadsheets and you have checked their answers, instruct them to save their documents as (*MultiSS*). You may also wish to have them print out a hard copy to use as a study guide.

This completes the lesson.

Lab #1 *(cont.)*

Multiplication Table

	A	B	C	D	E	F	G	H	I	J	K
1		1	2	3	4	5	6	7	8	9	10
2	1	1	2	3	4	5	6	7	8	9	10
3	2	2	4	6	8	10	12	14	16	18	20
4	3	3	6	9	12	15	18	21	24	27	30
5	4	4	8	12	16	20	24	28	32	36	40
6	5	5	10	15	20	25	30	35	40	45	50
7	6	6	12	18	24	30	36	42	48	54	60
8	7	7	14	21	28	35	42	49	56	63	70
9	8	8	16	24	32	40	48	56	64	72	80
10	9	9	18	27	36	45	54	63	72	81	90
11	10	10	20	30	40	50	60	70	80	90	100

Figure 5. Completed multiplication table spreadsheet

Lab #1 *(cont.)*

Notes:

_____

_____

_____

_____

_____

_____

_____

_____

_____

_____

_____

_____

_____

_____

_____

_____

_____

_____

_____

_____

_____

_____

_____

_____

_____

Lab #2 Introduction to Computer-Assisted Drawing: How to Read a Ruler

Purpose:

Students are introduced to the technical aspects of computer-assisted drawing by producing scale drawings which depict the different units of measurement on English and metric rulers.

Learning Objectives:

At the end of this lesson, each student will be able to:

- create a new drawing document.

- change a document's page orientation.

- change the viewing size of a document.

- utilize the horizontal and vertical rulers to draw objects to scale.

- use the **Rectangle** tool in a drawing.

- increase the thickness of a line in a drawing.

- alter the color of a line in a drawing.

- select specific objects in a drawing.

- group objects together in a drawing.

- move selected objects in a drawing.

- insert text into a drawing.

- change the size and color of text in a drawing.

- draw to scale the following units of measurement: eighth of an inch, fourth of an inch, half of an inch, one inch, and one centimeter.

Materials:

- *AppleWorks* (*ClarisWorks*), *Microsoft Word* for Macintosh or Windows, or any available drawing program

Lab #2 *(cont.)*

Procedure:

1. Begin this activity by explaining to your students the importance of using accurate measurements in the many aspects of technical drawing. Today, most technical plans and designs are created using a computer. This particular type of drawing is known as computer-aided or computer-assisted drawing, also called CAD. Architects, designers, engineers, and scientists all utilize computers to aid them in creating accurate drawings. Technical drawing is especially dependent on the use of accurate measurement, which includes the ability to draw to scale. Plans made from accurate-scale drawings can be used to build airplanes, automobiles, buildings, bridges, or homes. Instruct your class that they are going to create technical drawings that depict the different parts of a ruler.

2. Have your class create new drawing documents. If you are using *Microsoft Word*, go to the **VIEW** menu, select *Toolbars*, and choose the *Drawing* toolbar. In *AppleWorks* (*ClarisWorks*), simply open a new drawing document.

3. Next, they should choose the *Page View* from the **WINDOW** menu (*AppleWorks*) or *Page Layout* format from the **VIEW** menu (*Microsoft Word*) in order for them to see the margins of the page. They should also change the viewing size of the page to allow them to see the entire page on their screens. In *AppleWorks* (*ClarisWorks*), this is accomplished by clicking the **100** box located at the bottom left of their screen. They should reduce the size of their drawing to **67%**. In *Microsoft Word*, have them select the **VIEW** menu, choose *Zoom*, and change the view to **48%**.

4. Next, students should change the orientation of their pages. In *AppleWorks* (*ClarisWorks*), this is accomplished by selecting the **FILE** menu, choosing *Page Setup*, and then selecting the **Landscape**, or sideways, orientation. In *Microsoft Word*, they should choose the **FILE** menu, then select *Page Setup*, and click the **Paper Size** tab where they should alter the orientation to **Landscape**.

5. After they have adjusted their page orientation, they should show the ruler guides on their drawing document. In *AppleWorks* (*ClarisWorks*) this is accomplished by choosing the **WINDOW** or **VIEW** menu, depending on what version of *AppleWorks* (*ClarisWorks*) you are using, and selecting *Show Rulers*. In *Microsoft Word*, students should go to the **VIEW** menu and select *Ruler*. The students should now see vertical and horizontal rulers on their drawings. This is an essential part of technical drawing which facilitates drawing objects to scale.

Lab #2 *(cont.)*

6. Lastly, your students should set their margins in order to show as much of the printable page as possible. This is accomplished in *AppleWorks* (*ClarisWorks*) by choosing the **FORMAT** menu and then selecting ***Document***. They should set all four of their margins to (0.5) inches. If you are using *Microsoft Word*, choose the **FILE** menu and select ***Page Setup***. Then click the **Margins** tab, and change the top, bottom, and left margins to (0.5) inches, and the right margin to (0.63) inches. This should maximize the space utilized for their drawings while permitting them to keep the drawing within the printable area. Refer to Figures 1 and 2 to see the completed format for a simple technical drawing document.

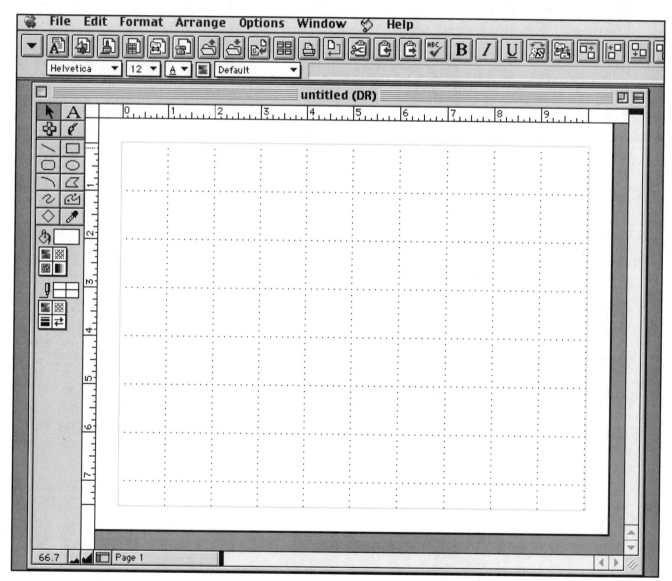

Figure 1. Completed formatting for a simple technical drawing using *AppleWorks* (*ClarisWorks*)

Lab #2 *(cont.)*

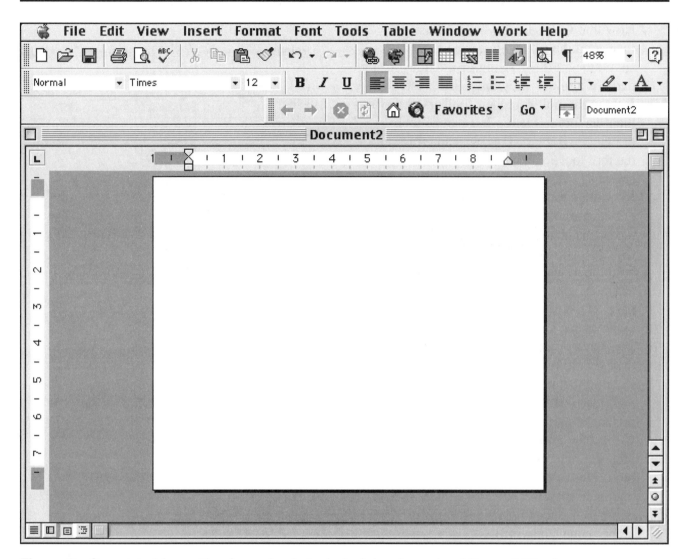

Figure 2. Completed formatting for a simple technical drawing using *Microsoft Word*

Lab #2 *(cont.)*

7. Now that your students have properly formatted their drawing documents, they should begin the drawing instructions for the parts of a ruler. They must first select the **Rectangle** tool from their toolbars and bring their cursors to the top-left part of their drawing. (Refer to Figures 3 and 4 for all of the tool locations that are required for this activity.) After they have selected the **Rectangle** tool, instruct them to locate the one-inch mark on the horizontal ruler at the top of the page. Once they are aligned with the one-inch mark, they should click and hold the mouse button down while they drag the rectangle towards the right side of their page. They should draw a rectangle that is eight inches long and one inch wide. When they have properly sized their rectangles, they should release the mouse button. Remind them to end the rectangle at the nine-inch mark on their horizontal rulers since the rectangle started at the one-inch mark. This will create a rectangle that is exactly eight inches in length. Explain to them that the rectangle they have just created will represent one inch; therefore, the scale that they are going to use for this assignment is eight inches equals one inch.

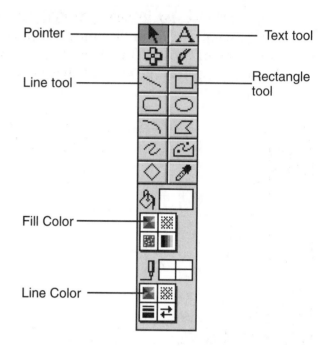

Figure 3. Required tools on the tool pallet for a *AppleWorks* (*ClarisWorks*) drawing document

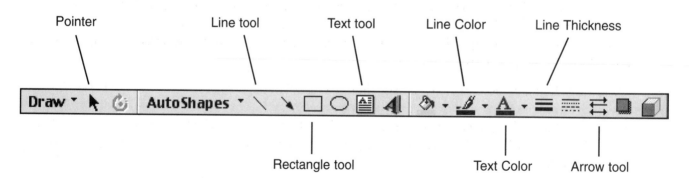

Figure 4. Required tools on the toolbar for a *Microsoft Word* drawing document

Lab #2 *(cont.)*

8. Next, explain to your students that they are going to change the line thickness of the rectangle that they just created. First, they must select the rectangle by choosing the selection tool, or Pointer, which resembles an arrow. Objects in a drawing are selected when students click them with the Pointer. They can tell when an object has been selected because its anchor points show. (See Figure 5.)

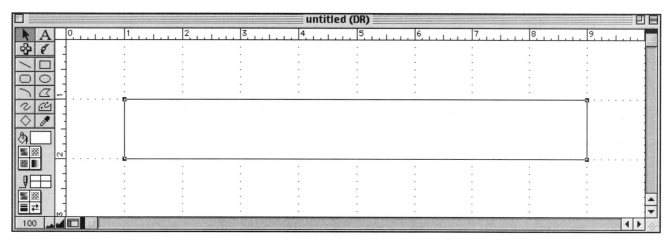

Figure 5. A selected object in a drawing showing the anchor points

9. Once your students have their rectangle selected, instruct them to choose the **Line Width** (*AppleWorks*) or **Line Style** (*Microsoft Word*) tool icon. It resembles a series of lines of varying thickness. Have them change the line thickness of their rectangle to **6-point**. Next, instruct your students to choose the **Line Color** tool icon, and have them change the color of the rectangle line to blue. Now they should label their rectangles with the correct scaled measurement it represents. In this case the blue rectangle will represent one inch. Have them select the **Text Box** (*Microsoft Word*) or **Text** (*AppleWorks*) tool, and add the label (*1 inch*) inside the rectangle near the upper right corner. Once they have created their labels, your students must increase the font size to **36 point**. In *AppleWorks* (*ClarisWorks*), this is accomplished by selecting the text with the pointer and choosing the **FORMAT** menu, then selecting *Size*, and *36Point*. If your class is using *Microsoft Word*, have them select their text with the pointer, choose the **FORMAT** menu and select *Font*, then change the size to *36*.

10. After your class has increased the size of their text labels, instruct them to change the color to blue. In *Microsoft Word* this is accomplished by selecting the text with the pointer and choosing the **Text Color** tool. In *AppleWorks* (*ClarisWorks*), choose the **FORMAT** menu, then select *Text Color*. The blue color students select should be the same shade of blue as the rectangle. The first part of the ruler is now complete.

Lab #2 *(cont.)*

11. Now your class should create the half-inch representation of a ruler. To do this, they should first draw another rectangle that is the same size as the first. Have them draw this rectangle about a half inch below the one they just created. They should select the **Rectangle** tool, begin at the one- inch horizontal ruler mark, and then drag to the nine-inch mark. The width of the rectangle should also be one inch, just like the first one. Once they have drawn their rectangles to the correct size, they must divide them in half. This is accomplished by using the **Line** tool. To properly divide the rectangle in half, they must locate the horizontal ruler mark at 5 inches. This should be the halfway mark on their rectangles. When they have located the halfway mark, have them use the **Line** tool to draw a small line that divides the new rectangle in half.

12. Before they increase the line thickness of the new rectangle, students must group the two objects together. Grouping joins two or more individual objects together to create one new object, making it easier to move within the drawing or change its appearance. To group objects together, students must hold down the **Shift** key on their keyboards while they select with the Pointer all of the objects that they want grouped. This will allow them to select multiple objects in their drawings. If using *AppleWorks* (*ClarisWorks*), students should go to the **ARRANGE** menu and select *Group*. In *Microsoft Word*, students should choose the **DRAW** menu located on the toolbar and select *Group*. All of the objects they have selected should now be grouped as one new object.

13. Instruct your students to group the second rectangle with the small line that divides it in half. Once these objects have been grouped, the class can increase the rectangle's line thickness to **6-point**. They should also change the line color to red. Then they must label the two halves accordingly. Ask your students what each part of the rectangle represents and how each section should be labeled. The first half of the rectangle should be labeled (*1/2 inch*), and the second half should be labeled (*2/2 inch*). Once the second rectangle is properly labeled, the class should also increase the font size to **36-point** and change the font color to **red**. Their drawings should now resemble the one in Figure 6.

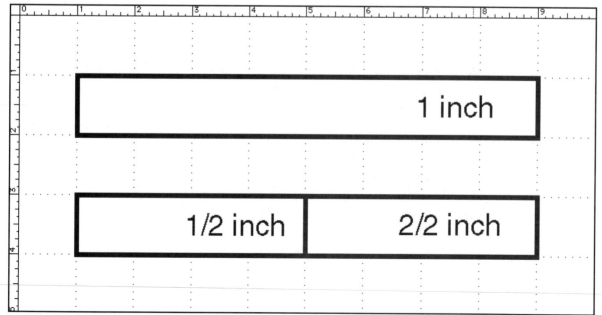

Figure 6. Second rectangle showing the half-inch sections of a ruler

20

Lab #2 *(cont.)*

14. Now your class is ready to draw a third rectangle. Have them draw this rectangle with the same dimensions that they used for the first two. The third rectangle is going to represent quarter inches on a ruler; therefore, once drawn, it must be divided into four sections. This is accomplished by using the **Line** tool to first draw one line dividing the rectangle in half, then another line dividing the two halves in half. Each section will then represent one-quarter of an inch. Once your students have created their quarter-inch sections, they must group all of the lines together with the rectangle.

15. Now your class should increase the line thickness of the new rectangle, and also change the line color to **green**. Once these changes have been made, they should label each section of the rectangle. Ask them how each section should be labeled. Beginning with the first section from the left, the labels should read (*1/4 inch*), (*2/4 inch*), (*3/4 inch*), and (*4/4 inch*). Remind your students to increase the size of the font to **36-point**. This time they should change the font color to **green**.

16. Next, your class needs to draw a fourth rectangle that will be divided into eight sections. This is easily accomplished by drawing a rectangle, dividing it in half using the **Line** tool, dividing the halves in half, then the quarters in half. This should divide the rectangle into eight equal sections. Your students should then group the lines with the rectangle, increase the line thickness to **6-point**, and change the line color to **purple**.

17. Now ask your class how these portions of the ruler should be labeled. Each section represents an eighth of an inch; therefore they should be labeled (*1/8 inch*), (*2/8 inch*), (*3/8 inch*), (*4/8 inch*), (*5/8 inch*), (*6/8 inch*), (*7/8 inch*), and (*8/8 inch*). Because of the smaller space available for labeling, the numbers should be typed above the inch labels. Do this by first typing the fraction, then pressing the **Return** or **Enter** key on the keyboard, and then typing the word (*inch*). The labels should then be increased to **36-point**, and their color should be changed to **purple**. Your students' drawings should now resemble the one in Figure 7.

Lab #2 *(cont.)*

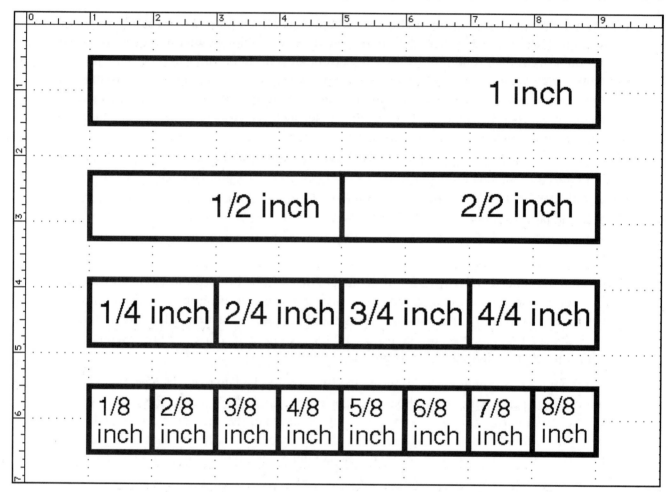

Figure 7. Four completed sections of an English system ruler

18. Next, explain to your students that some rulers are divided into even smaller sections, like sixteenths of an inch or thirty-fifths of an inch. This type of unit is needed for very precise measurement. Ask students what scale is used to represent one-eighth of an inch in their drawings. The answer should be that one inch equals one-eighth of an inch. Instruct your class to add a text box that shows the scale used for the drawing. Explain to them that all technical drawings require a visible scale key. They should locate the scale key in the bottom left part of their drawings.

Lab #2 *(cont.)*

19. Finally, explain to your students that the United States is unique—it utilizes two systems of measurement, the English system and the metric system. Ask them what the metric equivalent of the inch is. The answer should be the centimeter, which is the closest metric unit of measurement to the inch. There are 2.54 centimeters in an inch, which makes the centimeter roughly equal to 3/8 of an inch. Instruct your class to add one more rectangle to their drawings, this time to represent a centimeter. Ask them how big it should be. The answer is three inches long, which is 3/8 inch to scale. Have them draw this last rectangle below the fourth one and label it (*1 centimeter*). They must increase its line thickness and make it any color they choose. Once they have completed this last task, have them add their name to their drawings and save their documents as (*ruler*).

This completes the activity.

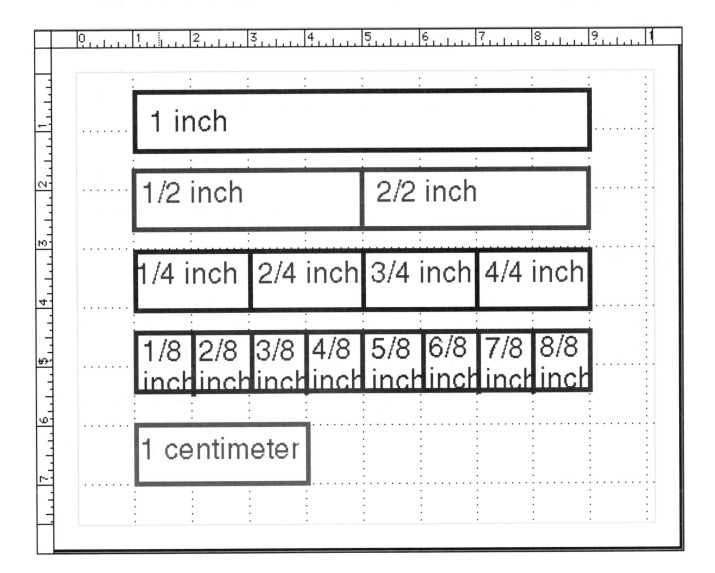

Lab #2 *(cont.)*

Notes:

_____

_____

_____

_____

_____

_____

_____

_____

_____

_____

_____

_____

_____

_____

_____

_____

_____

_____

_____

_____

_____

_____

_____

_____

_____

Lab #3 Introduction to Databases: Technology and Invention Database

Note: Because of the different features of *AppleWorks* (*ClarisWorks*) and *Microsoft Access*, this lesson is divided into two sections. The first section deals with using *AppleWorks* (*ClarisWorks*); and the second section, beginning on page 32, focuses on *Microsoft Access*.

Purpose:

Students are introduced to the basic setup and manipulation of the database application by creating simple databases containing an invention or technology for each letter of the alphabet.

Learning Objectives:

At the end of this lesson, each student will be able to:

- create a new database document.
- define fields for a new database.
- alter the format for a database record.
- enter the information into a database.
- create a new record.
- view the information in a database using different views.
- sort a database.
- search a database.
- work within two different applications at one time.
- utilize the Internet as a resource for locating specific information.
- identify twenty-six technologies, the name of their inventors, and what year they were invented.

Materials:

- *AppleWorks* (*ClarisWorks*) or *Microsoft Access* database applications
- Data Sheet from page 26
- Resource materials for additional technology and inventions

  The following Internet site contains excellent information on technological inventions and can be used as a resource for your students.

  American Inventors and Inventions

  http://www.150.si.edu/150trav/remember/amerinv.htm

Lab #3

Data Sheet

Invention or Technology	Year Invented	Inventor
Radio	1901	Marconi
Telephone	1876	Bell
Artificial Heart	Late 1970s	Jarvik
Sewing Machine	1850	Singer
Sugar Evaporation System	1843	Rillieux
Telegraph Key	1844	Morse
Telegraph	1832	Morse
Light Bulb	1879	Edison
Calculating Machine	1623	Schickard

Lab #3 *(cont.)*

AppleWorks (ClarisWorks) **Database Section**

Procedure:

1. Begin this lesson by explaining to your students the important role of databases in our society. Databases are used to store and organize information. One example of a database is the telephone book, which contains an enormous amount of information that is organized for ease of use. Another familiar database is the library card catalog. This database contains all of the information about what is available in the library. Explain to your class that both of the aforementioned databases are organized in a specific way that makes them easy to use. After you have discussed what a database is, explain to your class that they are going to create databases that will contain information about technology and inventions. Instruct your students that they are going to identify technologies or inventions for letters of the alphabet and enter this information into their databases. The data sheet for this lab can help them get started.

2. Have your students open new database documents in *AppleWorks* (*ClarisWorks*). The **Define Database Fields** window will appear. Explain to your students that a field is a category where information will be stored. For example, in a telephone book, the fields used might include last name, address, phone number, and others. Ask your students which fields might be used in a library card catalog database. Their answers should include author, title, subject, and Dewey decimal number. Students can then begin to define the fields for their databases. They should enter the first field in the **Field Name** box at the center of the window. The first field they will enter should be (*Letter of the Alphabet*). Once they type this field name, they should click the **Create** button. The field should now be displayed in the **Field Name** list at the top of the window.

3. To enter the next field, your students should press the **Delete** key on their keyboards. This will clear the **Field Name** box, and they can create the next field. The next field should be titled (*Technology or Invention*). They should then click the **Create** key to add this field to the field list. The next two fields to be created are (*Year Invented*) and (*Inventor*). If a student makes a spelling error or needs to remove a field from the field list, he or she should highlight the field to be removed in the field list and click the **Delete** button in the **Define Database Fields** window. Your students' field lists should resemble the one in Figure 1.

Lab #3 *(cont.)*

```
┌─────────────────────────────────────────────────────────────┐
│ ▦▦▦▦▦▦▦▦▦▦▦▦▦    Define Database Fields    ▦▦▦▦▦▦▦▦▦▦▦▦▦ │
├─────────────────────────────────────────────────────────────┤
│                                                             │
│  Field Name:                      Field Type:               │
│  ┌──────────────────────────────────────────────────────┐ │
│  │ Letter of the Alphabet          Text                 │▲│ │
│  │ Invention or Technology         Text                 │ │ │
│  │ Year Invented                   Text                 │ │ │
│  │                                                      │ │ │
│  │                                                      │ │ │
│  │                                                      │▲│ │
│  │                                                      │▼│ │
│  └──────────────────────────────────────────────────────┘ │
│                                                             │
│  Field Name: │Inventor         │   Field Type: │Text ▼│    │
│  ┌─────────────┐  ┌──────────┐  ┌──────────┐  ┌──────────┐ │
│  │   Create    │  │  Modify  │  │  Delete  │  │ Options… │ │
│  └─────────────┘  └──────────┘  └──────────┘  └──────────┘ │
│  ┌─┐  Type a field name and click Create, or select a field,│
│  │?│  make changes, and          ┌──────────┐              │
│  └─┘  then click Modify.         │   Done   │              │
│                                  └──────────┘              │
└─────────────────────────────────────────────────────────────┘
```

Figure 1. Completed define fields list for the Technology and Invention database

4. Now that your students have defined all of their fields, they should click the **Done** button in the **Define Database Fields** window. All of their fields should now be displayed in the form of a record. Explain to your class that a record is analogous to an index card that contains all of the field information for a particular item. Most databases are composed of hundreds, if not thousands, of records. Database records can be viewed in many different ways. For example, the view that your students currently have displayed is called the **Browse** view. This displays records much like an index card. This type of view is useful for displaying records that contain a lot of information. However, the **List** view is better used for this project. Instruct your students to open the **LAYOUT** menu and select *List*. Their databases should now be displayed as lists. The **List** view displays each record as a single line and makes it easier to input information into the database.

5. Once your students have changed to the **List** view, they should adjust the column width for each field so that the field labels can be easily read. This is accomplished by having students widen the columns as they might do in a spreadsheet application. Instruct your students to bring their cursors to the top row between two field names. Their cursors should change shape to a line with two arrows pointing outward. Your students should click and hold their mouse button down while they drag to the right until the field label is readable. Instruct your class to adjust the column width for each field.

Lab #3 *(cont.)*

6. Your students are now ready to begin filling in their fields with the first record. First, instruct your students to click into the blank cell below the **Letter of the Alphabet** field. Then they should enter the letter that will represent their first invention. In this case, it will be the letter (*R*). Explain to your students that they do not have to enter information into a database alphabetically since the database can sort records after the information is entered. After they enter the letter R into the **Letter of the Alphabet** field, instruct them to press the **Tab** key on their keyboards. This should move them into the next field of the first record. Explain to them that the invention they will enter into this field, which the letter R represents, will be the radio. After they type the word (*Radio*), they should move to the next field by pressing the **Tab** key again.

7. The next field requires the year that the invention was introduced. Ask your class if they know when the radio was invented. The radio was first successfully used in 1901, so instruct your class to type (*1901*) in the **Year Invented** field. The last field to be completed requires the name of the inventor of the radio. Ask your class if they know who invented the radio. Marconi, the father of the wireless telegraph, developed the first wireless form of communication, or the radio. Instruct your class to enter (*Marconi*) into the **Inventor** field. Your students' databases should now resemble the one shown in Figure 2.

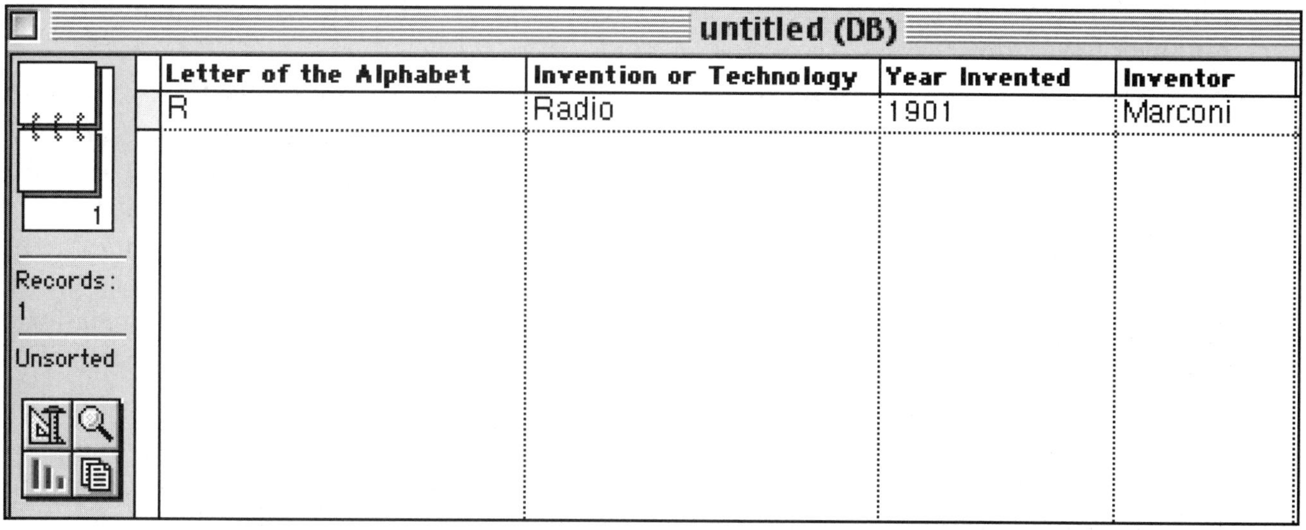

untitled (DB)

Letter of the Alphabet	Invention or Technology	Year Invented	Inventor
R	Radio	1901	Marconi

Records: 1
Unsorted

Figure 2. First completed record of the Technology and Invention database

Lab #3 *(cont.)*

8. Now that your class has completed all of the information for the first record, they should add another blank record to their databases. This is accomplished by selecting the **EDIT** menu and choosing *New Record*. A blank record should now appear below the first record. Your class should be able to enter their own information into the rest of the database. After they have completed all of the fields for a particular letter, remind them that they should add a new record.

9. Once all of your students have gathered enough information to complete at least ten records, instruct them to save their database documents as (*TechDB*). Explain to your class that they will be able to do more with their databases after you have explained more database functions, such as the sorting function. One of the advantages of storing information in a database is the ability to sort the information. The sorting function allows you to arrange information in a specific way. For example, a telephone book database is sorted alphabetically by a person's last name. This makes it easier to find the telephone number of a specific person. Explain to your students that they are going to use the sort function to arrange their database alphabetically. To do this, your students must go to the **ORGANIZE** menu, and select *Sort Records*. This should bring up the Sort Records window. Next, they should highlight the **Letter of the Alphabet** field in the **Field** list by clicking it. Now they should click the **Move** button, which will move the selected field to the **Sort Order** list. The **Ascending Order** button should also be selected, and then your class can click the **OK** button. Their database should now be sorted alphabetically by the **Letter of the Alphabet** field.

10. Now instruct your class to sort their databases by the **Year of Invention** field. This is accomplished by choosing the **ORGANIZE** menu and selecting *Sort Records*. Students should then highlight the **Letter of the Alphabet** field from the **Sort Records** list, and move it back into the **Field** list. Then they should select the **Year Invented** field and move it over to the **Sort Order** list. They should also choose the **Ascending Order** button and click the **OK** button. Explain to your class that the **Ascending Order** button sorts fields in ascending order, for example—A to Z or 1 to 10. The **Descending Order** button sorts fields in descending order, for example—Z to A or 10 to 1. Their database records should now be sorted from the oldest invention to the newest.

11. The other important database function your class will use is called the **Search** function. This allows them to search through their databases for specific information. Explain to your class that they are going to perform a search for all of the inventions created in the year 1901. This is accomplished by clicking the small magnifying glass icon to the left of the screen and choosing **New Search**. This will bring up the **Name for this search:** window. They should name this search (*1901*) and then click the **OK** button. This will bring up a blank record in the **Browse** view. Here your students should click the field in which they want to search for the specific information. They should click the **Year Invented** field box, enter (*1901*), and then press the **Return** key on their keyboards. This will return them to the **Browse** view, displaying all of the records in the database.

Lab #3 *(cont.)*

12. Now students should go to the **LAYOUT** menu and select *List*, which will return them to the **List** view. Explain to your class that sorting or searching a database should be done in the **List** view. Once your students return to the **List** view, they should click the magnifying glass icon once again. This time, their 1901 search should be included in the Search list. They should select **1901**, and all of the records that contain 1901 as the year invented will be displayed.

13. Next, explain to your class that in order to display all of the records in their entire database once again, they should go to the **ORGANIZE** menu and select *Show all Records*. Your class should now return to entering information into their databases.

This completes the introduction to database applications. Printing a database, along with other advanced assignments, will be covered in Lab #7.

Letter of the Alphabet	Invention or Technology	Year Invented	Inventor
R	Radio	1901	Marconi
T	Telephone	1876	Bell
A	Artificial Heart	late 1970's	Jarvik
S	Sewing Machine	1850	Singer
A	Antipolio Vaccine	1954	Salk
S	Sugar Evaporation System	1843	Rillieux
T	Telegraph Key	1844	Morse
T	Telegraph	1832	Morse
L	Light Bulb	1879	Edison
C	Calculating Machine	1623	Schickard

Figure 3. Complete Technology and Invention database.

Lab #3 *(cont.)*

Microsoft Access Section

Procedure:

1. Begin this lesson by explaining to your students the important role of databases in our society. Databases are used to store and organize information. One example of a database is the telephone book, which contains an enormous amount of information that is organized for ease of use. Another familiar database is the library card catalog. This database contains all of the information about what is available in the library. Explain to your class that both of the aforementioned databases are organized in a specific way that makes them easy to use. After you have discussed what a database is, explain to your class that they are going to create databases that will contain information about technology and inventions. Instruct your students that they are going to identify a technology or invention for each letter of the alphabet and enter this information into their databases. The Data Sheet for this lab can help them get started.

2. Instruct your students to open a new blank database document, give it the file name (*techdb*), and then click the **Create** button. They should be in the **Database** window. Have them create new tables into which they will input their information. Instruct your students to click the **New** button, select the **Datasheet View**, and click the **OK** button. They should now be looking at a blank table that resembles a spreadsheet. Ask your students to look along the top row at the labels that show the different fields. Explain to them that a field is a category under which information will be stored. For example, in a telephone book database, the fields used might include last name, address, phone number, etc. Ask your students what fields might be used in a library card catalog database. Their answers should include author, title, subject, and Dewey decimal number. Once you have discussed fields, students should begin to define the fields they will use for their databases. Defining fields simply means creating new field names that will best categorize their information. Instruct your class to click in the cell that is labeled **Field 1**, double-click to highlight the field name, and type (*Letter of the Alphabet*).

3. After your class has labeled the first field, have them press the **Enter** key on their keyboards. They will now have to adjust the column width so that the new label can be seen. Students should increase the width of the columns as they might do in a spreadsheet application. Instruct your students to bring their cursor up to the line between the **Letter of the Alphabet** label and **Field 2**. The cursor should change shape to a line with two arrows pointing outwards. When this occurs, they should hold down the mouse button and drag to the right until the entire label is visible. Now they are ready to change the label for the next field. **Field 2** should be changed to (*Invention or Technology*) and the column should be widened also. **Field 3** and **Field 4** should be changed to (*Year Invented*) and (*Inventor*) respectively.

Lab #3 *(cont.)*

4. Once your class has labeled all of the fields, explain that you will all fill in the first record together. Tell them the first letter of the alphabet they should use will be the letter R. (Explain to them that they do not have to enter information into a database alphabetically because it can be sorted later.) Instruct them to type the letter *(R)* into the first cell below the **Letter of the Alphabet** field. After they type the letter R into the correct location, instruct them to press the **Tab** key on their keyboards. This should move them to the next field. The invention they will use for the letter R will be the radio, so instruct them to type in the word *(Radio)* and then press the **Tab** key. Next, ask your class if they know when the radio was invented. The answer is *(1901)*, which is the year that will be entered into the **Year Invented** field. Finally, ask your class if they know who invented the radio. (Marconi invented the first use of wireless communication.) After they have entered *(Marconi)* into the last field, their database table should resemble the one in Figure 3.

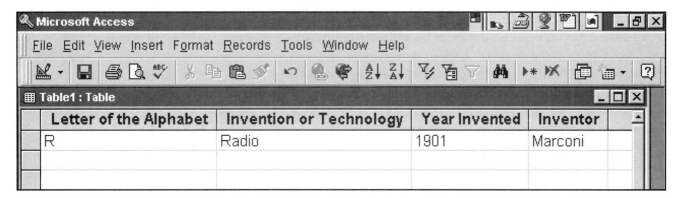

Figure 3. First completed record for the technology and invention database.

5. Now that your class has completed the first record, they can continue to fill in the fields for different letters of the alphabet. Once students have created at least ten records in their databases, ask them to stop working so you can explain more database functions. Instruct them to save their table by going to the **FILE** menu and selecting *Save As*. Have them use the filename *(techtable)*. After they have saved their tables, a message window will appear asking if they want to **Create a Primary Key**. A primary key assigns a number for each record. Instruct your students to click the **Yes** button.

Lab #3 *(cont.)*

6. One of the advantages of storing information in a database is the ability to sort that information. The sorting function allows you to arrange information in a specific way. For example, a telephone book database is arranged alphabetically, which makes it easy to locate information. Instruct your class that they are going to use the **Sort** function to arrange their database alphabetically. To do this, they must decide by which field they want to sort; in this case, they will arrange their database alphabetically by the **Letter of the Alphabet** field.

7. Instruct your class to click into the **Letter of the Alphabet** field, then choose the **RECORDS** menu, and select *Sort*. Then they must choose either **Sort Ascending** or **Sort Descending**. Sorting a field in ascending order will arrange items from A to Z or 1 to 10. Sorting fields in descending order will arrange items from Z to A or 10 to 1. Instruct your class to choose **Sort Ascending**. Their database tables should now be arranged alphabetically. Next, instruct your class to sort their databases by the **Year Invented** field in **Descending Order**. Once they have mastered the sort function, they can learn to search their database using the **Filter** function.

8. The ability to search a database for information makes it very easy to retrieve specific data contained in the records. Explain to your students that when they go to the library to find a book on a specific subject, they can use the library computer to search for this subject. This is the same type of "filtering" process that they will employ to locate information in their databases. Explain to your class that they are going to search their database for any technology that was invented in the year 1901. Have them choose the **RECORDS** menu and select *Filter*, and then choose *Filter by form*. Your class should now be looking at one record containing all blank fields. Instruct them to click the **Year Invented** field and type (*1901*). Next, they should choose the **FILTER** menu and select *Apply Filter/Sort*. All of the records of inventions in 1901 will now be displayed. Explain to your students that to display all of the records in their database once again, they must click the icon that resembles a funnel at the top of their screen, located to the left of the binocular icon. This button will remove the filter. The **Filter and Sort** buttons are shortcuts to using the functions mentioned in this lesson. See Figure 4 for more information about the identification of these buttons. Instruct your students to return to filling in the records for their databases.

This completes the introduction to database applications.

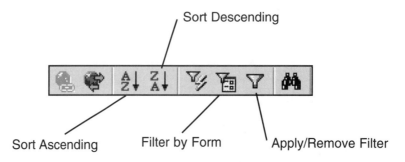

Figure 4. Shortcut buttons used for sorting and filtering a database in *Microsoft Access*

Lab #3 *(cont.)*

Notes:

_____

_____

_____

_____

_____

_____

_____

_____

_____

_____

_____

_____

_____

_____

_____

_____

_____

_____

_____

_____

_____

_____

Lab #4 Introduction to Spreadsheets: Human Population Growth

Note: Because of the different features of *AppleWorks* (*ClarisWorks*) and *Microsoft Excel*, this lesson is divided into two sections. The first section deals with using *AppleWorks* (*ClarisWorks*); and the second section, beginning on page 45, focuses on using *Microsoft Excel*.

Purpose:

Students enter data on human population for the past 2,000 years into a spreadsheet and create line charts.

Learning Objectives:

At the end of this lesson, each student will be able to:

- input column labels for a spreadsheet.
- format the columns for data entry in a spreadsheet application.
- enter data into spreadsheet cells.
- highlight the data in a spreadsheet.
- create a line chart using data entered into a spreadsheet.
- choose a chart type.
- label a chart's axis.
- create a title for a chart.
- alter the size of a chart.
- identify the time period when the Technological Revolution began.

Materials:

- *AppleWorks* (*ClarisWorks*) or *Microsoft Excel* spreadsheet application
- Data Sheet from page 37
- (*humanpop.cws*) *AppleWorks* (*ClarisWorks*) template or (*humanpop.xls*) *Microsoft Excel* template from the CD-ROM (optional)

   (If using a template, begin the lab with step 7.)

Lab #4 *(cont.)*

Data Sheet

Year (A.D.)	Population (Millions)
1	170
200	190
400	190
600	200
800	220
1000	265
1100	320
1200	360
1300	360
1400	350
1500	425
1600	545
1700	610
1750	760
1800	900
1850	1211
1900	1625
1950	2515
1996	5700
1998	5800

Lab #4 *(cont.)*

AppleWorks (*ClarisWorks*) **Spreadsheet Section**

Procedure:

1. Begin this lesson by explaining to your students that spreadsheet applications are an excellent tool for organizing data and graphically displaying it in the form of a chart or graph. This allows for better visualization of trends and relationships. Sometimes graphs and charts can also be used as prediction tools. Spreadsheet applications are widely used for this purpose in many different areas including business, science, engineering, and economics.

2. Instruct your students to open new spreadsheet documents in *AppleWorks* (*ClarisWorks*). Explain to your class that they are going to create spreadsheets that will contain data on human population growth for the past 2,000 years. Hand out a copy of the Human Population Growth data sheet to each student. Explain to them that in order to make data entry into a spreadsheet easier, it is important to create specific columns for each category of information. Remind your students that all spreadsheets are composed of columns and rows, and where a column meets a row is called a cell. Each cell has a specific address that corresponds to the specific column and row in which it is located. The cell location is displayed in the upper left part of the screen, making it easy to identify the cell that is active. Instruct your class to select cell A1 and input the first column label, (*Year A.D.*).

3. Instruct your students to press the **Tab** key on their keyboards to move them to cell B1. Now they should enter the label for column B, (*Population (Millions)*). Explain to them the importance of including the (*Millions*) labels. By adding this label, 2,000,000 can be entered simply as 2, thereby eliminating six zeros. This technique can be used to make data entry into a spreadsheet very efficient.

4. Now that students have entered the two column labels, have them widen the columns so that the labels are readable. This is accomplished by bringing the cursor up to the top of the spreadsheet, between column letters A and B. The cursor should change shape to a line with two arrows pointing outwards. (See Figure 1.) When this occurs, your students should click, hold the mouse button down, and drag to the right until the label can be seen completely. Have them repeat this procedure to widen column B also.

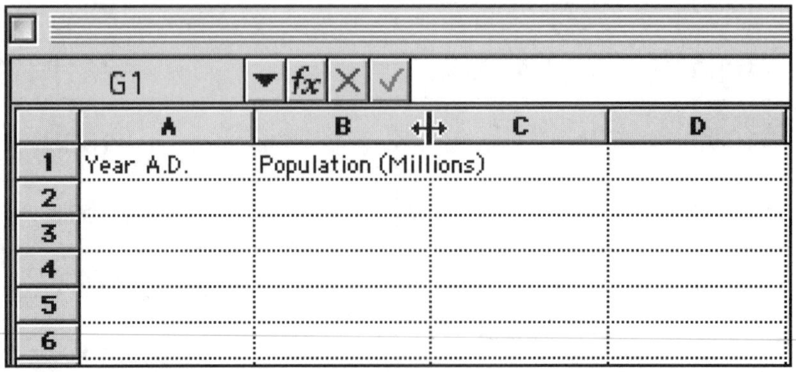

Figure 1. Adjusting the column width using the mouse

Lab #4 *(cont.)*

5. Instruct students to use the data provided from their worksheets to fill in the information for each column. Once they have finished entering the data into their spreadsheets, they should make additional changes to the format to make it easier to read. First, they should change the font style of the column labels to **Bold** in order to separate them more clearly from the data. Have them select the cell in which they want to make the changes, in this example cell A1, choose the **FORMAT** menu, then select *Style* and **Bold**. Repeat this procedure for the label in cell B1 also. After your students have changed the labels, it may be necessary to adjust the column width once again.

6. Next, your students should center all of the labels and data in each cell. To accomplish this, they should highlight only the cells that contain information. Instruct them to click in cell A1, then, while holding down the mouse button, drag and highlight all of the cells that contain information. Now they should go to the **FORMAT** menu, select *Alignment*, and choose *Center*. All of their data should now be centered.

7. Your class can now use the data that they have entered and formatted into their spreadsheets to create charts. To create a chart in *AppleWorks* (*ClarisWorks*), all of the data and labels to include in the chart must be highlighted. Your students should still have all of the data and column labels highlighted from their centering command. If they do not have their data highlighted, instruct them to do so. Stress the importance of this first step in creating a chart to avoid the "Not enough chart data" error message.

8. Direct students to go to the **OPTIONS** menu and select *Make Chart*. This action will open the **Chart Options** window, allowing them to create charts that best display the data contained in their spreadsheets. (See Figure 2.)

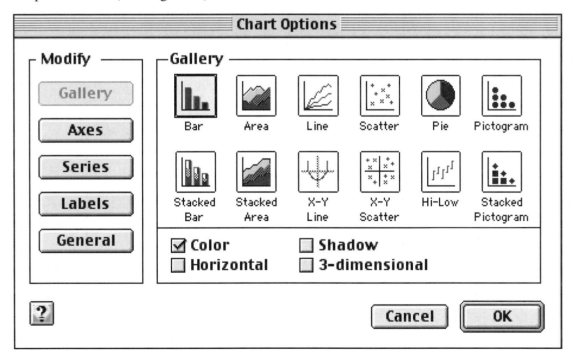

Figure 2. The Chart Options window in *AppleWorks* (*ClarisWorks*)

Lab #4 *(cont.)*

9. Instruct your class to create a line chart for their data by clicking the **Line Chart** icon. Next, they should click the **Axes** button, which will request the information required for the x and y axis of their charts. (See Figure 3.) Explain to your class that the x-axis represents the horizontal line of the chart, which is generally used to display time, and the y-axis represents the vertical line of the chart. For this line chart, they should only label the x-axis. Ask them what they believe the x-axis label should be. The answer should be "year." Instruct your class to click the **X axis** radio button at the top of the **Axis Chart Options** window and then type the label (*year*) into the **Axis Label** box.

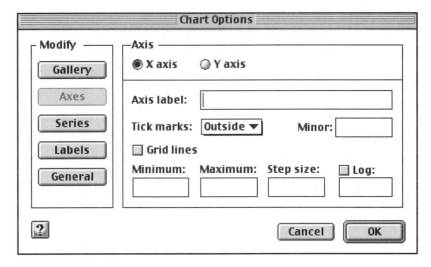

Figure 3. The Axes options of the Chart Options window

10. Next, instruct your class to click the **Series** button. The **Series** options will allow your class to choose a symbol that will represent their data points as they are plotted on the line chart (See Figure 4.) Instruct your class to choose any symbol they like by clicking it. They may also change the symbol's color by clicking the **Color** box located above the symbols.

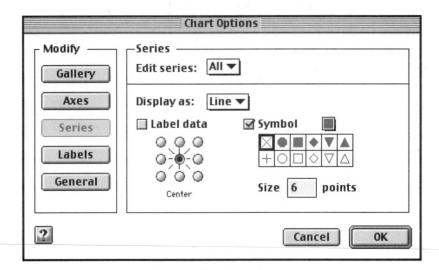

Figure 4. The Series options of the Chart Options window

Lab #4 *(cont.)*

11. Instruct your class to click the **Labels** button, which will allow them to create a label for their chart. Ask them what do they think the label should be. The chart label should be (*Human Population Growth*) and should be entered into the **Title** box. Finally, instruct your class to click the **General** button. This part of the **Chart Options** window is very important and somewhat complicated. Explain to your students that this window controls exactly what data will be displayed on their charts. The only data they should display is the population information. The year data will be used as a label only. In the **General Chart Options** dialog box, instruct your students to check the box next to **First** column under **Use numbers as labels in:**. (See Figure 5.) Your class should now be ready to display their formatted line charts. Instruct them to click the **OK** button.

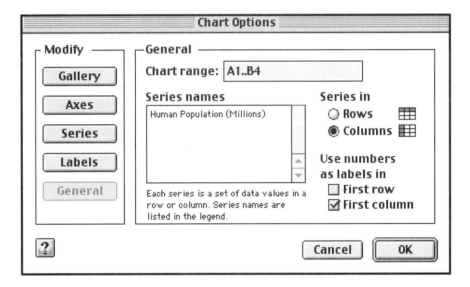

Figure 5. The General options of the Chart Options window

12. Explain to your class that more needs to be done to their line charts to make them easier to read and print. First, instruct them to choose the **WINDOW** or **VIEW** menu, depending on their version of *AppleWorks* (*ClarisWorks*), and select ***Page View***. This view will show the edges of the printable page and will make it easier for them to resize their charts. Next, have your class choose the **FILE** menu, and select ***Page Setup***. Here they should reorient their pages by choosing the Landscape orientation. Finally, instruct your students to go to the bottom left of their screens, click and hold their mouse buttons on the **100** button, and change the viewing size to **67%**. This will allow them to see an entire page with its margins. Your students' spreadsheets should now resemble the one in Figure 6.

Lab #4 *(cont.)*

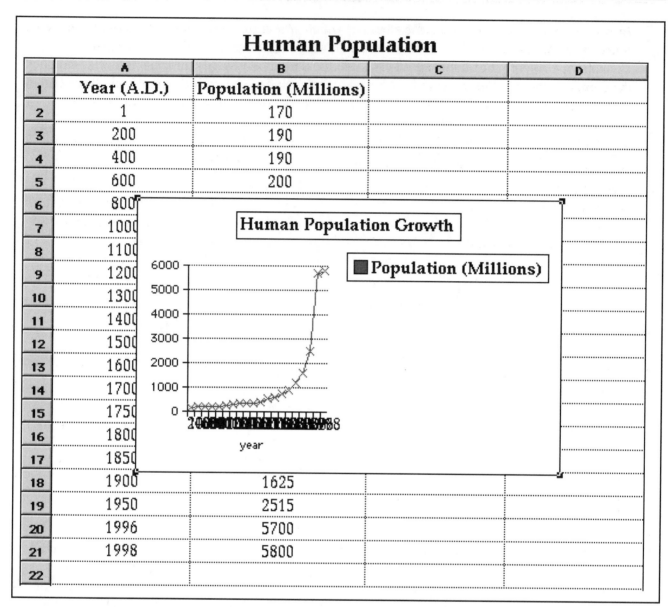

Human Population

	A	B	C	D
1	Year (A.D.)	Population (Millions)		
2	1	170		
3	200	190		
4	400	190		
5	600	200		
6	800			
7	1000			
8	1100			
9	1200			
10	1300			
11	1400			
12	1500			
13	1600			
14	1700			
15	1750			
16	1800			
17	1850			
18	1900	1625		
19	1950	2515		
20	1996	5700		
21	1998	5800		
22				

Figure 6. The Human Population Growth line chart ready to be re-sized

Lab #4 *(cont.)*

13. Now that your students have increased the size of their spreadsheet pages, they should enlarge the line chart so that it completely covers one page. To do this, they should use their cursor to select an anchor point corner of the chart. They should then hold down their mouse buttons and drag the corner of the chart to the edge of the page. They should repeat for the remaining three corners until the entire chart has been enlarged to the size of the page. Their charts should now be readable.

14. Students should insert headings at the top of their charts containing their names and the date. Instruct your students to go to the **FORMAT** menu and select *Insert Header*. Have them enter their first and last names and also the date. Their line chart for Human Population Growth is now complete. Ask your students to look at their charts and locate the point at which the population began to rise quickly. They should notice that this occurred shortly after 1850, the beginning of the Technological Revolution. Ask them how technology has affected human population. Also ask them to notice what happened to the population around 1400. (It lowered as a result of the black plague in Europe that killed one out of every three people.) Explain to your students that charts like this one can be used to illustrate many different points.

This completes the activity.

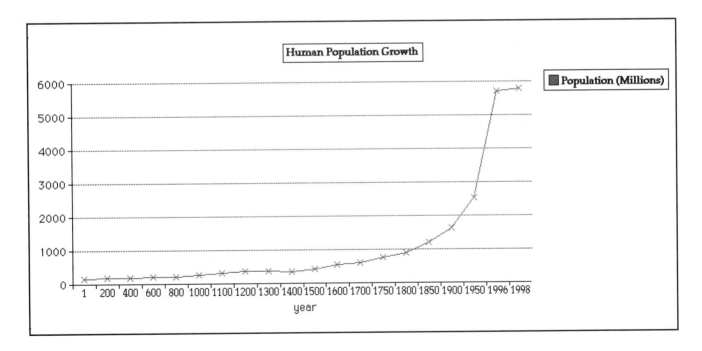

Lab #4 *(cont.)*

AppleWorks (*ClarisWorks*) Template for Lab #4

	A	B	C	D
1	Year (A.D.)	Population (Millions)		
2	1	170		
3	200	190		
4	400	190		
5	600	200		
6	800	220		
7	1000	265		
8	1100	320		
9	1200	360		
10	1300	360		
11	1400	350		
12	1500	425		
13	1600	545		
14	1700	610		
15	1750	760		
16	1800	900		
17	1850	1211		
18	1900	1625		
19	1950	2515		
20	1996	5700		
21	1998	5800		

Lab #4 *(cont.)*

Microsoft Excel Section

Procedure:

1. Begin this lesson by explaining to your students that spreadsheet applications are an excellent tool for organizing data and graphically displaying it in the form of a chart or graph. This allows for better visualization of trends and relationships. Sometimes graphs and charts can also be used as prediction tools. Spreadsheet applications are widely used for this purpose in many different areas including business, science, engineering, and economics.

2. Instruct your students to open new spreadsheet documents in *Microsoft Excel* (also called workbook documents). Explain to your class that they are going to create spreadsheets that will contain data on human population growth for the past 2,000 years. Hand out a copy of the Human Population Growth data sheet to each student. Explain to them that in order to make data entry into a spreadsheet easier, it is important to create specific columns for each category of information they are using. Remind your students that all spreadsheets are composed of columns and rows, and where a column meets a row is called a cell. Each cell has a specific address that corresponds to the column and row in which it is located. The cell location is displayed in the upper left part of the screen, making it easy to identify the active cell. Instruct your class to select cell A1 and input the first column label, (*Year A.D.*).

3. Instruct your students to press the **Tab** key on their keyboards to move them to cell B1. Now they should enter the label for column B into cell B1, (*Population (Millions)*). Explain to them the importance of including the (Millions) label. By adding this label, 2,000,000 can be entered simply 2, thereby eliminating six zeros. This technique can be used to make data entry into a spreadsheet very efficient.

4. Direct students to widen the columns so that the labels can be read. This is accomplished by bringing the cursor to the top of the spreadsheet, between the column letters A and B. The cursor should change its shape to a line with two arrows pointing outwards (see Figure 1). When this occurs, your students should click, hold the mouse button down, and drag to the right until the entire label can be seen. Repeat this procedure to widen column B as well.

5. Instruct students to enter into their spreadsheets the data from the data sheet. Once they have finished entering the data, they should make additional changes to the format to make it easier to read. First, they should change the font style of the column labels to bold in order to separate them more clearly from the data. Have them select cell A1 and click the **Bold** icon located on the toolbar. (See Figure 7.) The label should now be in bold font. Repeat this procedure for the label in cell B1. After your students have changed the labels, it may be necessary to adjust the column width once again.

Bold Icon   Center Alignment Icon

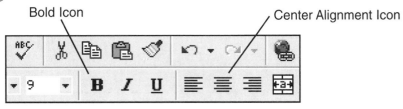

Figure 7. Bold and Center icons on the *Microsoft Excel* toolbar

Lab #4 *(cont.)*

6. Next, instruct your students that they should center all of the labels and data in each cell. To accomplish this, they should highlight only the cells that contain information. Instruct them to click cell A1, then while holding down the mouse button, drag to highlight all of the cells that contain information. Then they should choose the **Center Alignment** icon located on the toolbar. (See Figure 7.) All of the data should now be centered.

7. Your class should now use the data that they have entered and formatted into their spreadsheets to create charts. To create a chart in *Microsoft Excel*, they should use the **Chart Wizard**. To begin the **Chart Wizard**, they should go to the **INSERT** menu and select *Chart*. They can also click the **Chart Wizard** icon, which resembles a colorful bar graph and is located in the upper right section of the toolbar. The first option is the type of chart to use. Instruct them to choose a **Line** chart from the **Chart Type** list and use the default line chart that is already highlighted. (See Figure 8.) Your students should then click the **Next** button.

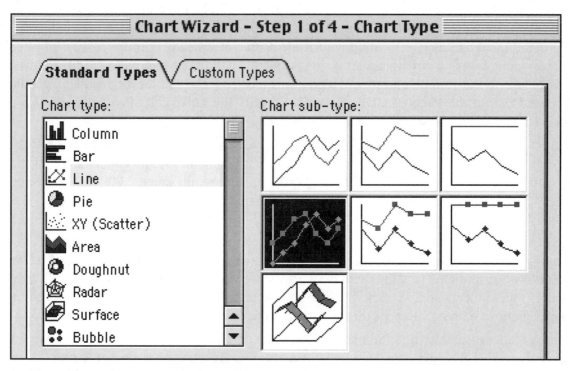

Figure 8. Line chart selection in the Chart Wizard

Lab #4 *(cont.)*

8. Now your students should choose the data range that will be displayed on their line charts. Have them locate the **Data Range** box, and at the end of this box they should select the small icon depicting a spreadsheet with a red arrow in the center. This will bring them back to their spreadsheet, where they should click and drag over the data they want displayed. In this example, they should drag over the data located in column B only, then press the **Enter** key on their keyboards. Next, your students should change the labeling for the x-axis by selecting the **Series** tab located at the top of the **Chart Wizard** window. Here they should select the data that will act as the x-axis label. Instruct them to click the red arrow icon located at the end of the **Category (x) axis label** box. This will return them to their data, where they should click and drag over only the numbers in the "Year" column. They do not need to include the Year label in column A, only the numbers. Once their data is selected, they can press the **Enter** key. Now they should click the **Next** button to take them to the next step of the **Chart Wizard**.

9. Next, your students should add a title to their charts. They should click in the **Chart Title** box and type (*Human Population Growth*). Once they enter their chart titles, they should press the **Tab** key on their keyboards, which will take them to the **X-axis Category Label** box . Have them type (*year*). Then they should click the **Next** button.

10. Finally, your students should select how to display their charts in their spreadsheet documents. For this example, they should click the **As New Sheet** button, and title it (*Line Chart*). Then they should click the **Finish** button. Their charts are complete and should resemble the one in Figure 9. Ask your class to look at their charts and locate the point at which the population began to rise quickly. This should be shortly after 1850, the beginning of the Technological Revolution. Ask them how technology has affected human population. Also ask them to notice what happened to the population around 1400. (It decreased as a result of the black plague in Europe that killed one out of every three people.) Explain to your students that charts can be used to illustrate many different points.

This completes the activity.

Lab #4 *(cont.)*

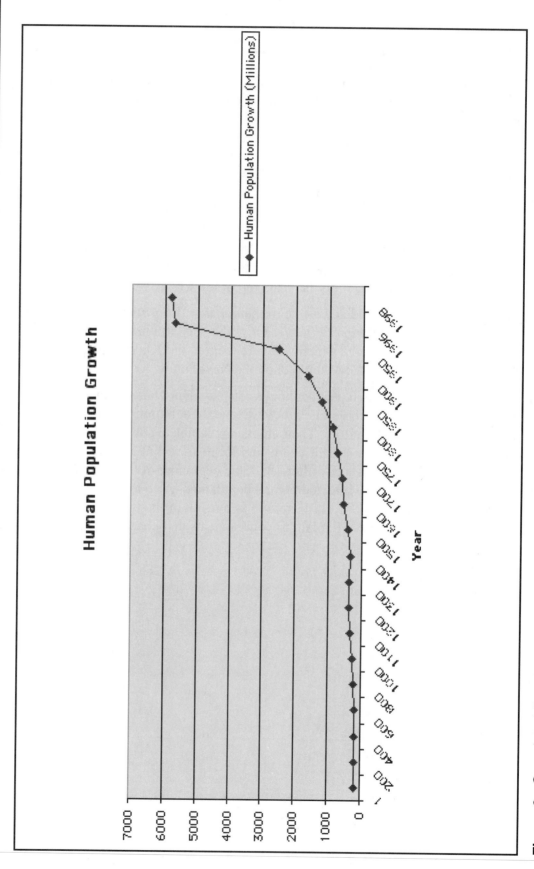

Figure 9. Completed line chart of human population growth using *Microsoft Excel*

Lab #4 *(cont.)*

Microsoft Excel Template for Lab #4

	A	B	C	D
1	Year (A.D.)	Population (Millions)		
2	1	170		
3	200	190		
4	400	190		
5	600	200		
6	800	220		
7	1000	265		
8	1100	320		
9	1200	360		
10	1300	360		
11	1400	350		
12	1500	425		
13	1600	545		
14	1700	610		
15	1750	760		
16	1800	900		
17	1850	1211		
18	1900	1625		
19	1950	2515		
20	1996	5700		
21	1998	5800		

Lab #5 Intermediate Spreadsheets: Water on Planet Earth

Note: Because of the different features of *AppleWorks* (*ClarisWorks*) and *Microsoft Excel*, this lesson is divided into two separate sections. The first section deals with using *AppleWorks* (*ClarisWorks*); and the second section, beginning on page 59, focuses on *Microsoft Excel*.

Purpose:

Students create pie charts to show the distribution of water on Earth. They use two sets of data from the same spreadsheet and display the two separate pie charts on the same page of the document.

Learning Objectives:

At the end of this lesson, each student will be able to:

- input column labels for a spreadsheet.
- format columns for data entry in a spreadsheet.
- enter data in the form of a percentage into spreadsheet cells.
- highlight data in a spreadsheet.
- display numbers in a cell as a percentage.
- create a pie chart using specific data entered into a spreadsheet.
- format a pie chart.
- create two charts from data entered into the same spreadsheet.
- display two charts on the same spreadsheet.
- alter the size of a chart.

Materials:

- *AppleWorks* (*ClarisWorks*) or *Microsoft Excel* spreadsheet application
- (*water.cws*) *AppleWorks* (*ClarisWorks*) template or (*water.xls*) *Microsoft Excel* template from the CD-ROM (optional)

  (If using the template, begin the lab with step 6.)

Lab #5 *(cont.)*

AppleWorks (*ClarisWorks*) **Spreadsheet Section**

Procedure:

1. Begin this lesson by explaining to your students that spreadsheet applications are an excellent tool for organizing data and displaying it graphically in the form of a chart or graph. Utilizing charts and graphs to display data allows you to better visualize trends and relationships that are occurring within your data. Pie charts are especially useful for displaying data that is in the form of a percentage.

2. Instruct your students to open new spreadsheet documents in *AppleWorks* (*ClarisWorks*). They should select cell A1, enter the label (*Geographic Area*), and press the **Tab** key. This will move them to cell B1. They will need to change the width of Column A in order to show the entire label. Remind them that to do this, they should move their cursor between columns A and B until the cursor changes to a line with two arrows pointing outwards. They should then click and drag to the right until the column is widened. After they have formatted column A, they should type the label (*Percentage of Planet*) into cell B1. The width of this column should also be increased.

3. Now students are ready to enter their data. Instruct them to click in cell A2, where they will enter (*Land*) as the first geographic area. After they enter this information, they should press the **Tab** key on their keyboards to move them into cell B2. Explain to your students that when they are entering data that represents a percentage into a spreadsheet, they must enter it in its decimal form. Tell them that approximately thirty percent of the planet is covered by land, and ask how this number would be entered into cell B2. The correct answer is (*.30*). They should enter this in cell B2.

4. Next, have them click in cell A3 and type (*Liquid Water*) as the next geographic location. They must then press the **Tab** key to move to cell B3. Explain to them that sixty-nine and three-tenths percent of the planet is covered in liquid water, and ask them how this should be entered into cell B3. The correct answer is (*0.693*), which they should enter into cell B3. The last geographic label should be entered into cell A4, and should be (*Ice*). Explain to your class that approximately seven-tenths of a percent of the planet is covered in ice. Ask them how this quantity should be entered into cell B4. The correct answer is (*0.007*).

Lab #5 *(cont.)*

5. Now that your students have entered all of their data, instruct them to change the style of their column labels to bold, and center all of the data in each cell. Explain to them that after they have altered the style of the font, they should readjust the column widths. Next, direct them to change the appearance of the numbers to better represent percentages. Have them highlight only the numbers located in column B. Remind them that this is accomplished by clicking and dragging over the cells they want to highlight. Instruct them to choose the **FORMAT** menu and select **Number**. This will bring up the **Format Number, Date, and Time** window. Here they should click the **Percent** button, then click the **OK** button. Their numbers should now be in the form of a percent, and their spreadsheets should resemble the one in Figure 1.

	A	B	C
1	Geographic Area	Percentage of Planet	
2	Land	30.00%	
3	Liquid Water	69.30%	
4	Ice	0.70%	
5			

Figure 1. Final cell format for the first pie chart in *AppleWorks* (*ClarisWorks*)

6. Explain to your class that they are going to use this data to create pie charts. Remind them that they should first highlight the cells that they want included in their charts. They should click into cell A1 and drag over only the cells that contain labels or data. After they have highlighted their data, they should choose the **OPTIONS** menu, and select *Make Chart*. They should now be looking at the **Chart Options** window, where they should select **Pie** from the **Chart Gallery**. They should also put a check mark next to the following options located at the bottom of the window: **Shadow**, **Scale Multiple**, and **Tilt**.

7. Direct students to click the **Series** button. In this window, students should put a check mark next to the **Label Data** box, then click the **% in both** button. Instruct your students to also put a check mark in the **Explode slice** box.

8. Next, they should click the **Labels** button. In this window, they should enter the chart title (*The Earth's Surface*) in the **Title** box. Students should click the **OK** button to display their charts.

Lab #5 *(cont.)*

9. Your class should be looking at their pie charts. There is still one more change to make. Notice that the sections of the pie are colored white, which makes them hard to see against a white background. Explain to them that they can change the background color of their pie charts with the **Fill Color** icon located on their toolbars.

10. To display their toolbars, they should choose ***Show Tools*** from the **WINDOW** menu. The **Fill Color** box is located just below the **Paint Can** icon. Instruct your class to click and hold the **Fill Color** box and change the background color of their chart to a light gray. Their pie chart should now resemble the one in Figure 2. Also explain to your students that if they want to make additional changes to their charts, they should simply double-click the chart and return to the **Chart Options** window.

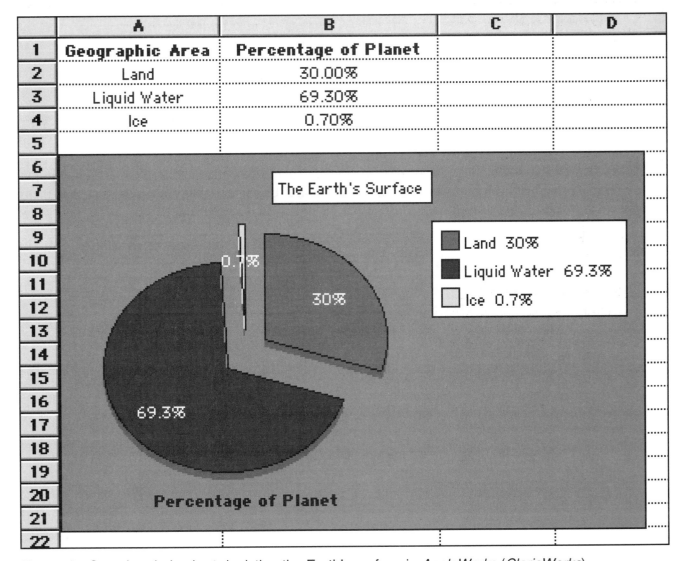

Figure 2. Completed pie chart depicting the Earth's surface in *AppleWorks* (*ClarisWorks*)

Lab #5 *(cont.)*

11. Next, explain to your students that they are going to add more data to their spreadsheets and create a second chart to show where the seventy percent of the water on the earth is located. Instruct them to click in cell A23, where they should type the label (*Location of Water*) and press the Tab key to move to cell B23. Then they should enter the label (*Percentage*). Now have them click into cell A24, type (*Oceans*), and press the **Tab** key to move to cell B24. Ask them if they know what percentage of the world's water the oceans hold. The correct answer is ninety-seven percent. Next, ask them how they should enter this data into the cell as a decimal. The correct answer is (*0.97*).

23	Location of Water	Percentage
24	Ocean	0.97
25		
26		
27		

Figure 3. More data entered into the *AppleWorks (ClarisWorks)* spreadsheet

12. Now your class should click in cell A25, where they should type the label (*Glaciers*). Explain to your class that one and one-tenth of a percent of the Earth's water is held in glacial ice. Ask them how they would enter this number as a decimal in cell B25. The correct answer is (*0.011*).

23	Location of Water	Percentage
24	Ocean	0.97
25	Glaciers	0.011
26	Groundwater	0.007
27	Lakes and Rivers	0.002

Figure 4. New data entered into the *AppleWorks (ClarisWorks)* spreadsheet.

Lab #5 *(cont.)*

13. The next set of data to be entered should be (*Groundwater*). Students should type this label in cell A26. Explain to your class that seven-tenths of a percent of the earth's water is underground. Ask them how should this be entered into cell B26. The correct answer is (*0.007*). The last row of data on the earth's water should represent how much is contained in Lakes and Rivers. This is the label for cell A27. The amount is two-tenths of a percent, which should be entered into cell B27 as (*0.002*).

14. Once this data has been entered into the proper cells, instruct your class to change the style of the labels in row 23 to bold, and center all of the data and labels. They should also change the format of the numbers to be displayed as percents. Remind them to highlight only the numbers, go to the **FORMAT** menu, select *Number*, and then choose **Percent** from the dialog box. Their spreadsheets should now resemble the one in Figure 5.

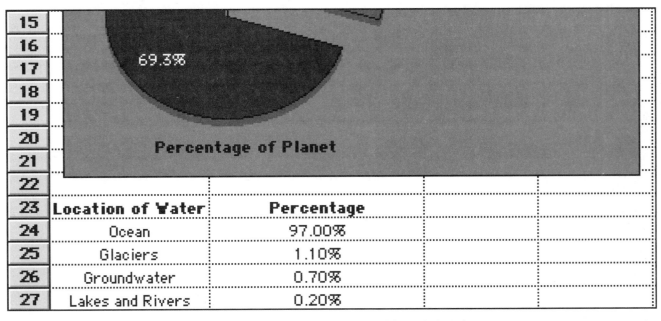

Figure 5. New data entered and formatted in *AppleWorks* (*ClarisWorks*)

Lab #5 *(cont.)*

15. Next, your students should highlight the new data, go to the **OPTIONS** menu, and select *Make Chart*. They should create a pie chart and put a checkmark next to the following options: **Color**, **Shadow**, **Scale Multiple**, and **Tilt**. They should then click the **Series** button, put a checkmark in the box next to **Label data**, and select **%** **in legend**. Also remind them to put a check mark in the **Explode slice** box. Next, they need to click the **Labels** button and title the chart (*Water on Earth*). Finally, your students should click **OK** to view their charts. They should reduce the viewing size of the entire document to **67%** so that both charts can be viewed on the screen. Remind your class that this is accomplished by clicking and holding the mouse button on the **100** button at the bottom left of their screen, and selecting **67%**. Then they should adjust the position of the second chart so that it is below the new data they entered. They may also resize each chart to fill one page. To do this, they should choose the **WINDOW** or **VIEW** menu, and select *Page View*. They can then drag the anchor points of their charts to make them larger and easier to read. Their spreadsheets should now resemble the one in Figure 6.

16. Instruct your class to choose the **FORMAT** menu and select *Insert Header* where they should enter their names and the date.

This completes the activity.

Lab #5 *(cont.)*

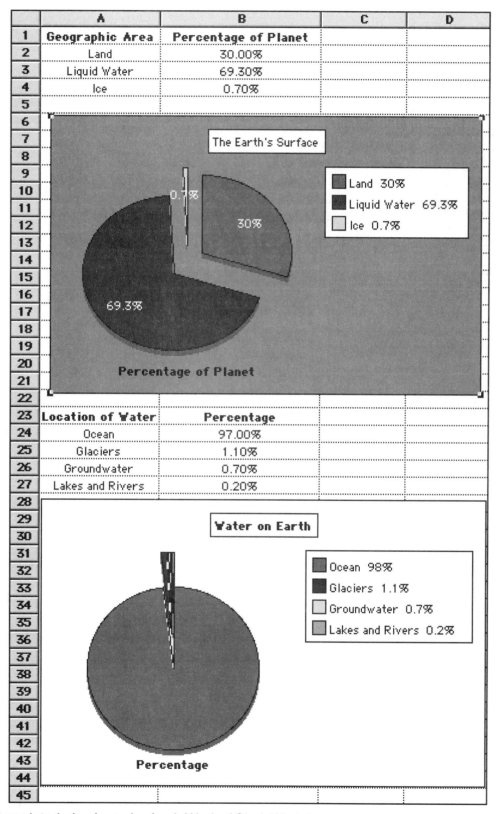

Figure 6. Completed pie charts in *AppleWorks* (*ClarisWorks*)

Lab #5 *(cont.)*

AppleWorks (*ClarisWorks*) Template for Lab #5

	A	B	C	D
1	**Geographic Area**	**Percentage of Planet**		
2	Land	30.00%		
3	Liquid Water	69.30%		
4	Ice	0.70%		
5				
6				
7				
8				
9				
10				
11				
12				
13				
14				
15				
16				
17				
18				
19				
20				
21				
22				
23	**Location of Water**	**Percentage**		
24	Ocean	97.00%		
25	Glaciers	1.10%		
26	Groundwater	0.70%		
27	Lakes and Rivers	0.20%		

58

Lab #5 *(cont.)*

Microsoft Excel Section

Procedure:

1. Begin this lesson by explaining to your students that spreadsheet applications are an excellent tool for organizing data and displaying it graphically in the form of a chart or graph. Utilizing charts and graphs to display data allows you to better visualize trends and relationships that are occurring within your data. Pie charts are especially useful for displaying data that is in the form of a percentage.

2. Instruct your students to open new workbook documents in *Microsoft Excel.* They should select cell A1, enter the label (*Geographic Area*), and press the **Tab** key. This should move them to cell B1. They will need to increase the width of column A in order to see the entire label. Remind them that to do this, they should move their cursors between columns A and B until the cursor changes to a line with two arrows pointing outwards. They should then click and drag to the right until the entire label can be seen. After they have widened column A, they should type the label (*Percentage of Planet*) into cell B1. The width of column B should also be adjusted.

3. Students are now ready to enter their data. Instruct them to click in cell A2, where they will type (*Land*) as the first geographic area. They should press the **Tab** key on their keyboard to move them to cell B2. Explain to your students that when they are entering data that represents a percentage into a spreadsheet, they must enter it in its decimal form. Instruct them that approximately thirty percent of the planet is covered by land, and ask how this number would be entered into cell B2. The correct answer is (*.30*). Instruct them to enter this into cell B2. Now, have them click into cell A3 and type (*Liquid Water*) as the next geographic location. They must then **Tab** to move to cell B3. Explain to them that sixty-nine and three-tenths percent of the planet is covered in liquid water, and ask them how this should be entered into cell B3. The correct answer is (*0.693*), which they should enter into cell B3. The last geographic label should be entered into cell A4, and should be (*Ice*). Explain to your class that approximately seven-tenths of a percent of the planet is covered in ice. Ask them how this quantity should be entered into cell B4. The correct answer is (*0.007*).

4. Instruct students to change the style of their column labels to bold, and center all of the data in each cell. Explain to them that after they have altered the style of the font, they should readjust their column widths. They should also change the appearance of the numbers to better represent percentages. Have them highlight only the numbers located in column B. Then they can choose the **FORMAT** menu, select *Cells*, and click the **Number** tab. Here they should click **Percentage** under the **Category** list, then click the **OK** button. Their numbers should now be in the form of a percent, and their spreadsheets should now resemble the one in Figure 7.

Lab #5 *(cont.)*

	A	B
1	**Geographic Area**	**Land**
2	Land	30.00%
3	Water	69.30%
4	Ice	0.70%
5		

Figure 7. Correctly formatted data for the first pie chart in *Microsoft Excel*

5. Your students are now ready to use the **Chart Wizard** to create their first pie charts. Remind them to open the **Chart Wizard** by going to the **INSERT** menu and selecting ***Chart***, or clicking the **Chart Wizard** icon located on the toolbar. They should select **Pie** from the **Chart Type** list, then choose the **Exploded pie with the 3-D visual effect** option. Then they should click the **Next** button.
6. Now your students can select the data range that they want displayed in their chart. They should click the red arrow icon located at the right end of the **Data Range** box. This will bring them back to their spreadsheets, where they should click and drag over the cells they want displayed in their chart. In this example, they should select all of the cells that contain data and labels. Once this is accomplished, they should press the **Enter** key on their keyboards and click the **Next** button.
7. In this next window, students should click the **Titles** tab and type (*The Earth's Surface*) in the **Chart Title** box. Then they should click the **Data Labels** tab and select **Show label and percent**. Your students should now click the **Next** button. In this window, students should click the **As object in Sheet 1** button. They should then click the **Finish** button to view their charts. Their spreadsheets should now resemble the one in Figure 8.

	A	B	C
1	**Geographic Location**	**Percentage of Planet**	
2	Land	30%	
3	Water	69%	
4	Ice	1%	

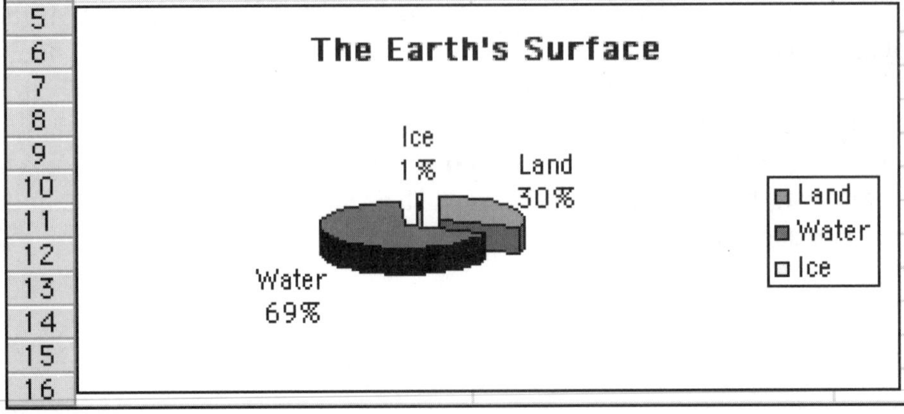

Figure 8. First completed pie chart using *Microsoft Excel*

Lab #5 *(cont.)*

8. Next, explain to your students that they are going to add to their spreadsheets data which they will use to create a second chart. Explain to your class that they are going to enter data into their spreadsheet that shows exactly where the water that composes ninety-seven percent of the earth is located. Instruct them to click into cell A18, where they should type the label (*Location of Water*) and press the **Tab** key to move them to cell B18. In this cell, they should type the label (*Percentage*).

9. Now have them click into cell A19, where they should type (*Oceans*) and press the **Tab** key to move them into cell B19. In this cell they should enter the percentage of water on the earth that is located in the oceans. Ask them if they know what percentage of the world's water the oceans hold. The correct answer is ninety-seven percent. Next, ask them how they should enter this data into the cell as a decimal. The correct answer is (*0.97*).

10. Now your class should click into cell A20, where they should type (*Glaciers*) as the label. Explain to your class that one and one-tenth of a percent of the earth's water is held in glacial ice. Ask them how they would enter this number as a decimal into cell B20. The correct answer is (*0.011*).

11. The next set of data to be entered should be (*Groundwater*). They should enter this label into cell A21. Explain to your class that seven-tenths of a percent of the earth's water is held under ground. Ask them how should this be entered into cell B21. The correct answer is (*0.007*). The last row of data on the earth's water should represent how much is contained in (*Lakes and Rivers*). This is the label for cell A27, and the amount is two-tenths of a percent, which should be entered into cell A22 as (*0.002*).

12. Once this data has been entered into the proper cells, instruct your class to change the style of the labels in row 18 to bold, and center all of the data and labels. They should also change the format of the numbers to display them as a percentage. Remind them to highlight only the numbers, then choose the **FORMAT** menu, select *Cells*, click the **Number** tab, and choose **Percentage** in the **Category** list. They should then click the **OK** button. Their data should now be in the form of a percent.

13. Instruct your class to use the data they have just entered to create a pie chart that is formatted like the first one. Remind them to use the **Chart Wizard**. At the **Data Range** window, they should select only the new data. They should also title this chart (*Water on Earth*). Allow your students to format their chart by themselves, and assist only when needed.

Lab #5 *(cont.)*

14. The second chart should resemble the one in Figure 7. Notice that the labels do not show on this chart. This is due to the smaller pie slice sizes. Did your students discover this potential problem? You may wish to have them choose the **None** option in the **Data Labels** tab of the **Chart Wizard**. Remind your students they can always change the chart appearance by double-clicking the chart to select it and then choosing the **Chart Wizard** button. This will enable them to make changes to an already existing chart.

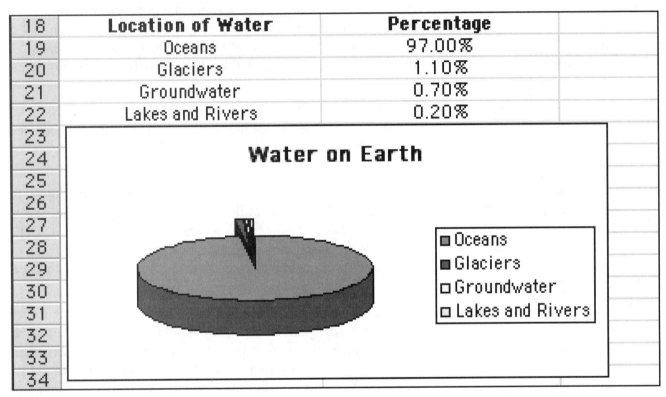

Figure 7. The second completed pie chart located below the first chart in Sheet 1 of *Microsoft Excel*

The activity is now complete.

Lab #5 *(cont.)*

Microsoft Excel Template for Lab #5

	A	B	C	D
1	**Geographic Location**	**Percentage of Planet**		
2	Land	30%		
3	Water	69%		
4	Ice	1%		
5				
6				
7				
8				
9				
10				
11				
12				
13				
14				
15				
16				
17				
18	**Location of Water**	**Percentage**		
19	Oceans	97.00%		
20	Glaciers	1.10%		
21	Groundwater	0.70%		
22	Lakes and Rivers	0.20%		

Lab #6 Intermediate Computer-Assisted Drawing: National Weather Maps

Purpose:

Students are introduced to the use of computer-assisted drawing as they create accurate weather forecast maps. The use of computerized forecast models to predict changes in weather is an increasingly important technological tool. Students use a drawing application program to generate accurate weather maps that contain current national weather conditions.

Learning Objectives:

At the end of this lesson, each student will be able to:

- create a new drawing document.
- change the viewing size and page orientation of a document.
- utilize the horizontal and vertical rulers to draw objects to scale.
- import and alter the size of a graphic in a drawing.
- insert text into a drawing.
- change the size and color of text in a drawing,
- move selected objects in a drawing.
- increase the size and alter the color of a line in a drawing.
- group objects together in a drawing.
- utilize the **Oval** tool, **Line** tool, and **Arrow** tool in a drawing.
- utilize the **Copy** and **Paste** function in a drawing.
- utilize the **Free Rotate** option in a drawing.
- identify and draw the following weather map symbols: Cold Front, Warm Front, Low Pressure, and High Pressure.

Materials:

- *AppleWorks* (*ClarisWorks*) or *Microsoft Word* for Macintosh or Windows, or any available drawing program
- A current national weather map. This is available in most newspapers or can be downloaded from the Internet.
- (*map.jpg*) JPEG template file from the CD-ROM to import into a drawing document

Lab #6 *(cont.)*

Procedure:

1. Begin this activity by explaining to your students the importance of using computer technology to create accurate forecast weather maps. The use of computers has greatly improved our national weather network by providing valuable, if not life saving, warnings all around the nation. Explain to your class that they are going to create accurate forecast maps for the nation's weather using computer-assisted drawing.

2. Instruct your class to open new drawing documents. If your students are using *Microsoft Word*, they should click the **VIEW** menu, select *Toolbars*, and then choose the **Drawing** toolbar. In *AppleWorks (ClarisWorks)*, they should open **Drawing** documents. Next, they should choose the **Page Layout** or **Page View** format in order to allow them to see the margins of their pages. They should also change the viewing size of their pages so that they can see the entire page on their screens. In *AppleWorks (ClarisWorks)*, this is accomplished by clicking on the **100** box located at the bottom left-hand side of the screen. They should reduce the size to **67%**. In *Microsoft Word*, have them select the **VIEW** menu, choose *Zoom*, and change the view to **48%**.

3. Next, your students should change the orientation of their pages. In *AppleWorks (ClarisWorks)*, this is accomplished by going to the **FILE** menu, choosing *Page Setup*, and then selecting the **Landscape** (or sideways) orientation. In *Microsoft Word*, go to the **FILE** menu, select *Page Setup*, and choose the **Paper Size** tab to alter the orientation to **Landscape**. After they have adjusted the page orientation, students should show the ruler guides on their drawing documents. In *AppleWorks (ClarisWorks)*, this is accomplished by choosing the **WINDOW** or **VIEW** menu, depending on what version of *AppleWorks (ClarisWorks)* you are using, and selecting *Show Rulers*. In *Microsoft Word*, choose the **VIEW** menu, and select *Ruler*. The students should now see a vertical and horizontal ruler on their drawing pages. This is an essential part of technical drawing and makes it easier to draw objects to scale.

4. Finally, your students should change their margins in order to use as much as the printable page as possible for their drawings. This is accomplished in *AppleWorks (ClarisWorks)* by choosing the **FORMAT** menu, then selecting *Document*. All four margins should be set to (0.5) inches. If they are using *Microsoft Word*, they should go to the **FILE** menu, select *Page Setup*, and choose the **Margins** tab. Then they can change the top, bottom, and left margins to (0.5) inches and the right margin to (0.63) inches. This should maximize the space available for their drawings. Refer to Figure 1 to see the completed format for a simple technical drawing document.

Lab #6 *(cont.)*

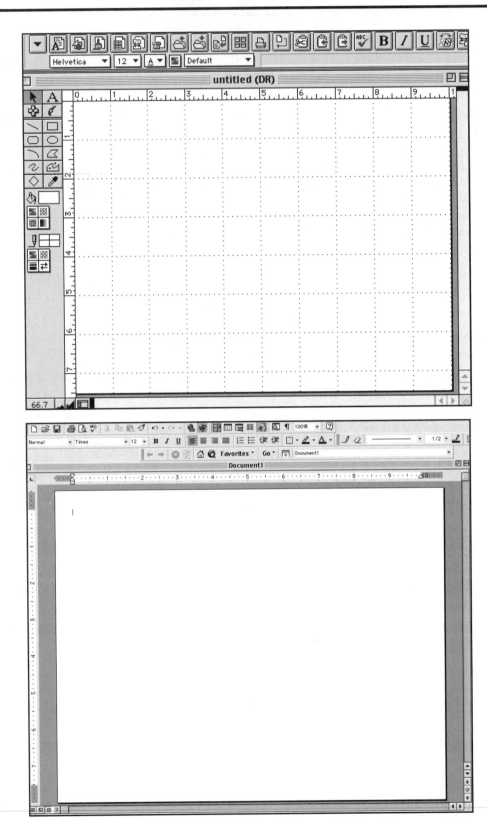

Figure 1. Completed formatting for a simple technical drawing using *AppleWorks* (*ClarisWorks*) (top), and *Microsoft Word* (bottom).

Lab #6 *(cont.)*

5. If students are using *AppleWorks* (*ClarisWorks*), instruct them to choose the **OPTIONS** menu and select ***Turn Autogrid Off***. This will make it easier for them to place objects in their drawings. Next, students should import the (*map.jpg*) file into their drawings. This file contains an outline of the United States (minus Alaska and Hawaii) for them to use as a background for their weather maps. To import this graphic into their *AppleWorks* (*ClarisWorks*) drawing documents, students should go to the **FILE** menu and choose *Insert*. If your class is using *Microsoft Word*, they should go to the **INSERT** menu, choose *Picture*, and select **From File**. They must then locate the file on their hard drive or disk, select it, and then import it into their drawings. In *Microsoft Word*, they must choose the **Float over text option** before clicking the **Import** button.

6. Next, your students should enlarge the map outline to fit within the page of their drawings. This is accomplished by clicking and dragging each of the map's corner anchor points to the corners of the page. Once this is accomplished, their maps should resemble the one in Figure 2.

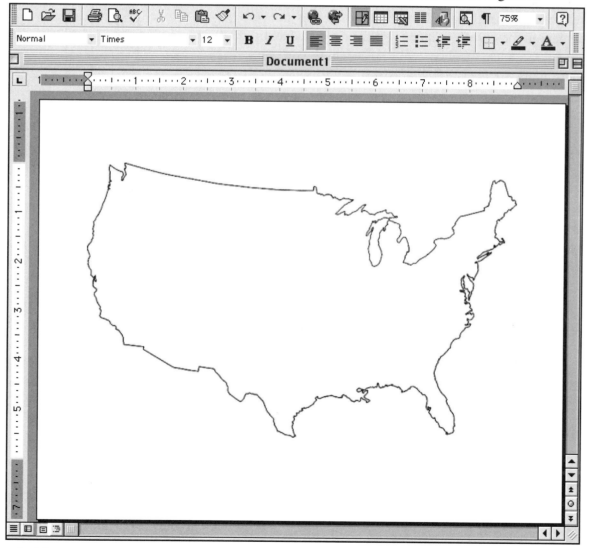

Figure 2. The National Map graphic inserted and re-sized in a *Microsoft Word* document

Lab #6 *(cont.)*

7. Next, instruct your students that the first items they should add to their maps are the pressure centers. Meteorologists use pressure systems to track areas of bad weather and areas of fair weather. Areas of high pressure usually are associated with good weather, and areas of low pressure are associated with bad weather. Explain to your class that there are two symbols that meteorologists use to identify these pressure centers on their maps. A blue "H" represents a high pressure, and a red "L" represents a low pressure. Students should look on the reference map that they are using and locate all of the low-pressure centers around the United States. They can use the horizontal and vertical rulers as reference points to help them locate these pressure centers in the correct locations on their maps. Next, students can use the **Text** tool to place an (L) on their maps where each low pressure center is.

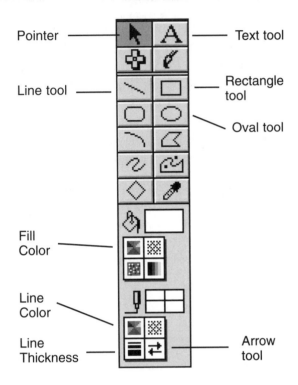

Figure 3. The *AppleWorks* (*ClarisWorks*) Drawing toolbar

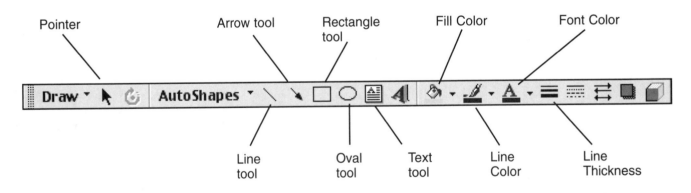

Figure 4. The *Microsoft Word* Drawing toolbar

Lab #6 *(cont.)*

8. Once your students have placed the low-pressure centers in the right locations on their maps, instruct them to increase the size of each L to **46-point** and change the font color to **red**. Remind your students that they must first use the Pointer to select the letter before the font size can be increased. Next, they should look for the areas of high pressure on the reference map and place an (*H*) on their maps for each location. Once the high-pressure symbols have been properly placed, instruct your students to increase the font size of each H to **46-point** and change the font color to **blue**. Their maps should now resemble the one in Figure 4 (although the specific locations of the pressure centers will depend on the national weather at the time of your lesson).

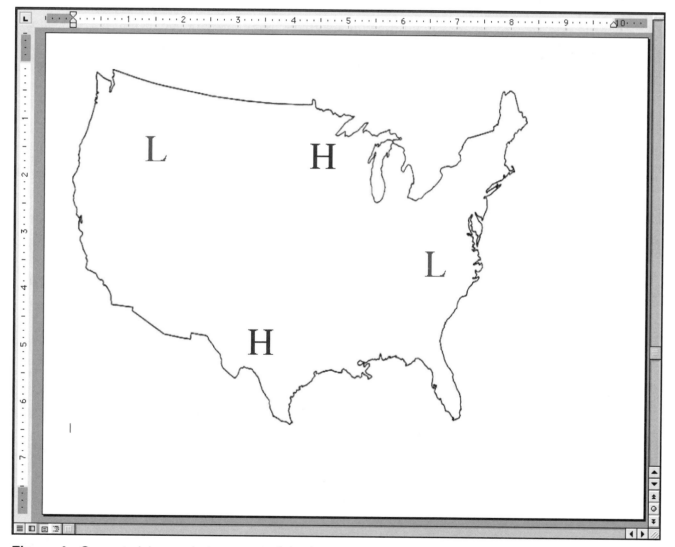

Figure 4. Correct sizing and placement of the low and high pressure symbols on the weather map

Lab #6 *(cont.)*

9. Now that your class has added all of the pressure centers to their maps, they should draw the weather fronts. Fronts are areas where two different air masses come together. For this exercise, you should explain to your class that the two basic fronts are cold fronts, which bring cold air into an area; and warm fronts, which bring warm air into an area. Explain to your class that fronts are usually attached to areas of low pressure. To draw the front symbols, your students will need to draw individual objects and group them together. Instruct your class to scroll down to the bottom of their maps to a blank area in which they can draw their first front symbols.

10. Explain to your students that a cold front is depicted on a weather map as a thick blue line with blue arrows showing the direction in which the front is moving. To draw a cold front symbol, students first use the **Line** tool to draw a horizontal line approximately one inch in length. Once they have drawn this line, they should use the **Line Thickness** tool to increase its thickness. Then, instruct them to use the **Line Color** tool to change the color of the line to blue.

11. Next, your students should add three arrows pointing downward from the line. Instruct them to return to the 100% view to make it easier for them to add their arrows. To add the arrows in *AppleWorks* (*ClarisWorks*), students should use the **Line** tool to draw a small line approximately one-half inch in length, and increase its line thickness to **6-point**. Next, they should use the **Arrow** tool and choose the **Arrow At End** option to add an arrow. Then, they should change the line color to **blue**. To create an arrow in *Microsoft Word*, they should select the **Arrow** tool and draw a small line approximately one-half inch in length. They should then use the **Line Style** tool to increase the line thickness to **6-point** and use the **Line Color** tool to change the color to **blue**.

12. Now, they should attach the blue arrow to the blue line. They will need to add another arrow to the line. The easiest way to do this is to have them copy the arrow they just created. They should click to select it, go to the **EDIT** menu, and then choose *Copy*. Then they should go to the **EDIT** menu again and select *Paste*. A copy of the arrow will appear in their drawings, and they will need to move it into position. They should then paste a third arrow and attach it to the line to complete their cold front symbols. See Figure 5 for an example of a cold front symbol.

Figure 5. Cold front symbol using a blue line grouped with three blue arrows

Lab #6 *(cont.)*

13. Next, instruct your students to group together the three arrows with the blue line to form one new object. Explain to your class that grouping makes it easier to move objects in a drawing that contains many parts. To group objects together, your students should hold down the **Shift** key on their keyboards while they use the Pointer to select the objects that they want to be grouped together—the three arrows and the blue line. If using *AppleWorks* (*ClarisWorks*), they should choose the **ARRANGE** menu, and select *Group*. In *Microsoft Word*, they should go to the **DRAW** menu on their toolbars, and select *Group*. The cold front objects should now be grouped and can be easily moved.

14. Tell your students that they will now create the warm front symbol, which is depicted as a red line with half circles pointing in the direction of the front's movement. Instruct your students to draw a small line approximately one inch in length and increase its thickness to **6-point**. Then they should change the color of the line to red. To make the half circles, students should can use the **Oval** tool to draw an oval approximately one-quarter of an inch wide. They should then change the line color and fill color of the oval to **red**. Next, they should click and drag the oval so that it is attached to the red line. (See Figure 6.) They should select the red oval they just created, copy it, and then paste it into their drawings. Then they can reposition the new red oval on the line and repeat the paste process again to create a third red oval. Once their warm front symbol resembles the one in Figure 6, they can group it together to form one object.

Figure 6. Warm front symbol created using a red line and grouped with three red ovals

15. Now your students are ready to place the front symbols on their map. They should first locate on their reference map where the fronts are and decide where they need to be placed on their map. For example, if there is a warm front associated with a low pressure center, students should select their warm front symbol with the Pointer, copy it, then paste it into their drawing. Then they can drag the symbol to its proper location.

Lab #6 *(cont.)*

16. It may be necessary for students to rotate their front symbols to orient them in the correct direction. This is done in *AppleWorks* (*ClarisWorks*) by going to the **ARRANGE** menu and selecting *Free Rotate*. Students can then click one of the anchor points and rotate the symbol to the correct orientation on their map. If students are using *Microsoft Word*, they should choose the **DRAW** menu, select *Rotate* or *Flip*, then choose **Free Rotate**. They can then click the symbol and rotate it to the correct orientation. Once the object is in the correct position, they should select **Free Rotate** again to cancel the option. Most fronts will be much longer than the individual symbols, so instruct your students to copy and paste front pieces together, aligning them to make the front symbol the correct length. Once your students have added all of their warm fronts, they should use the same technique to add the cold fronts. Their map symbols should resemble the symbols in Figure 7.

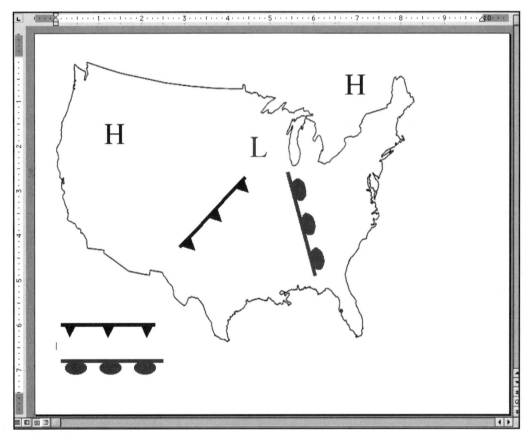

Figure 7. Placement of warm and cold front symbols using copy and paste and the free rotate option

17. If time allows, have your students use the **Text** tool to add some of the regional temperatures to their maps. Your students may add text of other information, such as indicating where it may rain or snow and where there are sunny or cloudy conditions. There are many variations that can be included into this type of activity, depending on the time you have to spend on it. You can even create weather maps that are specific for your state or a particular region of the country.

The activity is now complete.

Lab #6 *(cont.)*

Notes:

_____

_____

_____

_____

_____

_____

_____

_____

_____

_____

_____

_____

_____

_____

_____

_____

_____

_____

_____

_____

_____

_____

_____

_____

Lab #7 Intermediate Databases: Major Agricultural Crops of the United States

Note: Because of the differences that exist in setting up a database in *AppleWorks* (*ClarisWorks*) and *Microsoft Access*, this lesson is divided into two sections. The first section deals with using *AppleWorks* (*ClarisWorks*); and the second section, beginning on page 82, focuses on *Microsoft Access*.

Purpose:

Students create databases consisting of thirty-two important agricultural crops grown in the U.S. They use their agricultural databases to search for and generate printed reports of specific information.

Learning Objectives:

At the end of this lesson, each student will be able to:

- create a new database document.
- define fields within a database.
- create a new record in a database.
- enter information into a database.
- alter the format of a database record.
- utilize different record viewing options for the database.
- sort the records in a database.
- search for specific information within a database.
- generate and print a report containing information contained within a database.

Materials:

- *AppleWorks* (*ClarisWorks*) or *Microsoft Access* database applications
- Data Sheet from page 75
- Agricultural Database Work Sheet from page 76
- (*crops.cws*) *AppleWorks* (*ClarisWorks*) template or (*crops.mdb*) *Microsoft Access* template from the CD-ROM (optional)

  [If using the template file, start the lesson with step 12 in the *AppleWorks* (*ClarisWorks*) section and step 8 in the *Microsoft Access* section]

Lab #7 *(cont.)*

Data Sheet

Common Name	Use	Scientific Name	Family	Agronomic Classification
Wheat	Flour	Triticum vulgare	Grass	Small Grain
Oats	Feed, Food Grain	Avena sativa	Grass	Small Grain
Barley	Feed, Malt	Hordeum vulgare	Grass	Small Grain
Rye	Feed, Flour, Pasture, Cover	Secale cereale	Grass	Small Garin
Rice	Food Grain	Oryza sativa	Grass	Small Grain
Corn	Feed, Silage, Food Grain, Oil, Sugar, Starch, Industry	Zea mays	Grass	Grain, Oil Seed
Soy Beans	Feed, Food, Oil	Glycine max	Legume	Oil-Seed
Sorghum	Feed, Silage	Sorghum vulgare	Grass	Grain
Cotton	Textiles, Oil	Gossypium hirsutum	Mallow	Fiber, Oil-Seed
Alfalfa	Hay, Pasture, Cover	Medicago sativa	Legume	Forage
Sweet Clover	Pasture, Cover	Melilotus alba	Legume	Forage
Red Clover	Hay, Pasture, Cover	Trifolium pratense	Legume	Forage
White Clover	Hay, Pasture, Silage, Cover	Trifolium repens	Legume	Forage
Trefoil	Hay, pasture, Cover	Lotus tenius	Legume	Forage
Timothy	Hay, Pasture, Cover	Phleum pratense	Grass	Forage
Orchard Grass	Hay, Silage, Pasture	Dactylis glomerata	Grass	Forage
Smooth Brome Grass	Hay, Silage, Pasture	Bromus inermus	Grass	Forage
Kentucky Bluegrass	Turf, Pasture	Poa pratensis	Grass	Forage
Bermuda Grass	Turf, Pasture	Cynodon dactylon	Grass	Forage
Tall Fescue	Hay, Pasture	Festuca elatior	Grass	Forage
Annual Lespedeza	Hay, Pasture, Cover	Lespedeza striata	Legume	Forage
Sudan Grass	Hay, Silage, Pasture	Sorghum vulgare	Grass	Forage
Foxtail Millet	Hay	Setaria italica	Grass	Forage
Buckwheat	Flour	Fagopyrum esculentum	Buckwheat	Grain
Canola	Oil, Industry	Brassica napus	Mustard	Oil-Seed
Dry Beans	Food, Feed	Phaseolus vulgaris	Legume	Oil-Seed
Flax	Oil, Linen, Straw	Linum usitatissium	Flax	Oil and Fiber
Peanuts	Oil, Food	Arachis hypogaea	Legume	Root and Sugar
Sugar Beets	Sugar, Feed	Beta vulgaris	Goosefoot	Oil-Seed
Sunflower	Oil, Food	Helicanthus annuuss	Composite	Oil-Seed
Sugar Cane	Sugar	Saccarum officinarum	Grass	Sugar
Tobacco	Smoking, Chewing, Medicine, Pesticides	Nicotania tabacum	Nightshade	Special

Lab #7 *(cont.)*

Agricultural Database Work Sheet

Follow the directions to sort and search for information in your agricultural database.

1. Sort your database alphabetically by the common name of the crop.

2. Search your database for all crops that are used for silage, and write the common name of each below:

   _____

   _____

   _____

   _____

   _____

3. Print a list containing all of the crops in the legume family.

4. Using the Search function, determine how many crops are grown in the United States to

   make hay. _____

5. Using the Search function, determine how many crops are used by industry. _____

   _____

6. Using the Search function, determine how many crops are grown in the U. S. for oil.

   _____

7. Print a list of all crops used for cover.

Lab #7 *(cont.)*

AppleWorks (*ClarisWorks*) **Database Section**

Procedure:

1. Begin this activity by explaining to your students the important role that agriculture plays in our society. United States agriculture is the most advanced in the world. This often-overlooked aspect of our nation's economy is responsible for feeding millions of people around the world by developing and utilizing advanced techniques for producing food. All U.S. citizens should appreciate the food and fiber system that provides them with the highest standard of living on the planet. One of science's most important topics is the role that biotechnology plays in supporting our nation's agriculture. Biotechnology is the use of living organisms to perform a task or produce a product. Today's modern agriculture encompasses many different biotechnologies, including plant science, genetic engineering, beneficial insects, and cultured bacteria. Explain to your class that they will create a database that catalogs thirty-two important crops grown in the United States that support our powerful economy. Students will then use their databases to answer a series of questions that pertain to agriculture.

2. Have your students open new database documents in *AppleWorks* (*ClarisWorks*). The **Define Database Fields** window will appear. Remind your students that a field is a category under which that information will be stored. They should enter (*Common Name*) as the first field in the **Field Name** box at the center of their window, then click the **Create** button. The field should now be displayed in the **Field Name** list at the top of the window.

3. To enter the next field, students should press the **Delete** key on their keyboards to clear the **Field Name** box and type (*Use*). They should then click the **Create** button to add this field to the field list. The next three fields to be created are (*Scientific Name*), (*Family*), and (*Agronomic Classification*). Remind your students if they make a spelling error or need to remove a field from the field list, they should highlight the field to be removed in the field list and click the **Delete** button in the **Define Database Fields** window. When they have completed defining their fields, the students' field list should resemble the one in Figure 1.

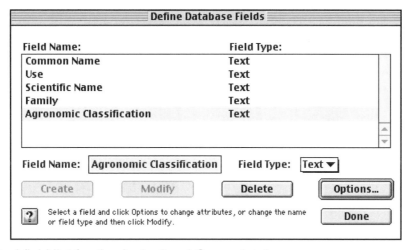

Figure 1. Completed field list for the Agricultural Crops database

Lab #7 *(cont.)*

4. Now that your students have defined their fields, they should click the **Done** button in the **Define Database Fields** window. All of their fields should be displayed in the form of a record. Remind your class that a record is analogous to an index card that contains all of the information for a particular item. Most databases are composed of hundreds, if not thousands, of records. Database records can be viewed in many different ways. The view that students should currently have showing is called the **Browse** view. This displays records much like an index card. This type of view is useful for displaying records that contain a lot of information. However, the **List** view is better for use with this project.

5. Instruct your students to open the **LAYOUT** menu, and select *List*. Their databases should now be displayed as lists. The **List** view displays each record as a single line and makes it easier to input information.

6. Once your students have changed to the **List** view, they should adjust the column width for each field so that the field labels can be easily read. This is accomplished much like changing column width in a spreadsheet application. Students should bring their cursors up to the top row between two field names. When their cursors change to a line with two arrows pointing outward, they should click and hold their mouse buttons while dragging to the right until they can see the entire field label. Instruct your class to adjust the column width for each field.

7. Your students should now begin to fill in the fields for their first record. First your students should click into the blank cell below the **Common Name** field. Then they should enter (*wheat*) as the name of the first crop and press the **Tab** key on their keyboards. This should move them into the next field of the first record. Your class should now identify how wheat is used in the **Use** field. In this case its main use is for flour. After they have typed (*flour*), they should move to the next field by pressing the **Tab** key.

8. The next field requires the **Scientific Name** for the crop. Ask your class if they know why it is important for plants to have scientific names. The answer is that scientific names provide a universal way to identify plants. Researchers all over the world use scientific names for this purpose. The common names are often different in each country, which makes it difficult to identify specific plants. The scientific name for a plant contains its genus and species name. Students should type (*Triticum vulgare*) in this field.

Lab #7 *(cont.)*

9. After your students have entered the scientific name for wheat, they should move to the next field and enter the **Family Classification**. Knowing to which the family a crop belongs is important in order to determine how crops are related to one another. This can be significant information because the same insects or diseases might affect plants that are in the same family. Therefore, controlling these problems might be similar for a whole family of crops. They should enter (*grass*) in the **Family Classification** field.

10. The **Agronomic Classification** field identifies how a crop is used in our society and how it relates to our nation's economy. Some crops are grown for industrial uses, while others are primarily for feed. This classification helps track the potential market for specific crops. Students should type (*Small Grain*) in the **Agronomic Classification** field. The first record is completed and should resemble the one shown in Figure 2.

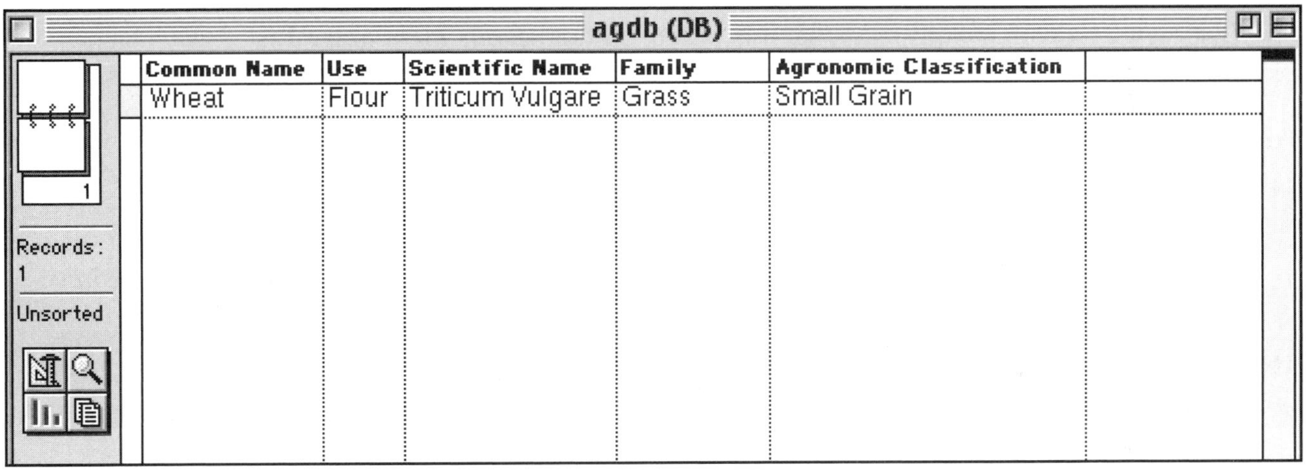

Common Name	Use	Scientific Name	Family	Agronomic Classification	
Wheat	Flour	Triticum Vulgare	Grass	Small Grain	

Records: 1
Unsorted

Figure 2. First completed record of the Agricultural Crops database

11. Now that your class has completed all of the information for the first record, it is time to add another blank record to their database. This is accomplished by selecting the **EDIT** menu, and choosing *New Record*. A blank record should appear below the first record. Students will need copies of the Data Sheet for this lab in order to know the information to enter into the rest of the database. When they have complete all of the fields for a particular crop, they should add a new record. After your students have completed ten complete records, instruct them to save their database documents as (*AGDB*). Explain that they will be able to complete their databases after you have demonstrated some additional database functions.

12. One of the advantages of storing information in a computer database is the ability to sort it. The sorting function allows you to arrange information in a specific way. Explain to your students that they should use the **Sort** function to arrange their database alphabetically. To do this, students should go to the **ORGANIZE** menu and choose *Sort Records*. This will bring up the **Sort Records** window. Next, they should select the **Common Name** field in the field list and click the **Move** button, which moves the selected field into the **Sort Order** list. The **Ascending Order** button should also be selected before they click the **OK** button. Their database should now be sorted alphabetically by the first letter of the **Common Name** field.

Lab #7 *(cont.)*

13. Another important database function your class will use is called the **Search** function. This allows students to search through their databases for specific information. Tell your class that they should perform a search for all of the crops that are used for silage. Explain to them that silage is chopped corn packed in silos or bunkers where it ferments and becomes preserved. The silage is then used as feed for cattle. Instruct your class to conduct a search for silage by clicking the small magnifying glass icon to the left of their screen and choosing **New Search**. This will bring up the **Name for this search** window. They should name this search (*silage*), then click the **OK** button. This will bring up a blank record in the **Browse** view. Here your students should click in the field in which they want to search for the specific information. They should click into the **Use field** box, and enter (*silage*), then press the **Return** key on their keyboards. This will return them to the **Browse** view and display all of the records in their databases.

14. Next, students should choose the **LAYOUT** menu and select *List*, which will return them to the **List** view. Explain to your class that it is best to sort or search while in the **List** view. Once students return to the **List** view, they should click the magnifying glass icon again, and this time their search name, silage, should be included in the **Search list**. They should select this search, and all of the records that contain silage will be displayed.

15. Explain to your class that if they want to print the results of their search, also known as a report, they should go to the **FILE** menu and select *Print*. Remind them that before they print out their reports, they should insert a heading that contains their names and the date. To insert a heading, they must go to the **FORMAT** menu and select *Insert Header*.

16. Next, explain to your class that in order to display all of the records in the entire database again, they should go to the **ORGANIZE** menu and select *Show All Records*. Your class should continue to complete their databases and then use them to perform the functions and answer the questions included on the Agricultural Database Work Sheet.

This completes the activity.

Lab #7 *(cont.)*

AppleWorks (*ClarisWorks*) Template for lab #7

Crops (lab7) (DB)

Records: 32
Unsorted
31

Common Name	Use	Scientific Name	Family	Agronomic Classification
Wheat	Flour	Triticum vulgare	Grass	Small Grain
Oats	Feed, Food Grain	Avena sativa	Grass	Small Grain
Barley	Feed, Malt	Hordeum vulgare	Grass	Small Grain
Rye	Feed, Flour, Pasture, Cover	Secale cereale	Grass	Small Garin
Rice	Food Grain	Oryza sativa	Grass	Small Grain
Corn	Feed, Silage, Food Grain, Oil, Sugar, Starch,	Zea mays	Grass	Grain, Oil Seed
Soy Beans	Feed, Food, Oil	Glycine max	Legume	Oil-Seed
Sorghum	Feed, Silage	Sorghum vulgare	Grass	Grain
Cotton	Textiles, Oil	Gossypium hirsutum	Mallow	Fiber, Oil-Seed
Alfalfa	Hay, Pasture, Cover	Medicago sativa	Legume	Forage
Sweet Clover	Pasture, Cover	Melilotus alba	Legume	Forage
Red Clover	Hay, Pasture, Cover	Trifolium pratense	Legume	Forage
White Clover	Hay, Pasture, Silage, Cover	Trifolium repens	Legume	Forage
Trefoil	Hay, pasture, Cover	Lotus tenius	Legume	Forage
Timothy	Hay, Pasture, Cver	Phleum pratense	Grass	Forage
Orchard Grass	Hay, Silage, Pasture	Dactylis glomerata	Grass	Forage
Smooth Brome	Hay, Silage, Pasture	Bromus inermus	Grass	Forage
Kentucky Bluegrass	Turf, Pasture	Poa pratensis	Grass	Forage
Bermuda Grass	Turf, Pasture	Cynodon dactylon	Grass	Forage
Tall Fescue	Hay, Pasture	Festuca elatior	Grass	Forage
Annual Lespedeza	Hay, Pasture, Cover	Lespedeza striata	Legume	Forage
Sudan Grass	Hay, Silage, Pasture	Sorghum vulgare	Grass	Forage
Foxtail Millet	Hay	Setaria italica	Grass	Forage
Buckwheat	Flour	Fagopyrum	Buckwheat	Grain
Canola	Oil, Industry	Brassica napus	Mustard	Oil-Seed
Dry Beans	Food, Feed	Phaseolus vulgaris	Legume	Oil-Seed
Flax	Oil, Linen, Straw	Linum usitatissium	Flax	Oil and Fiber
Peanuts	Oil, Food	Arachis hypogaea	Legume	Root and Sugar
Sugar Beets	Sugar, Feed	Beta vulgaris	Goosefoot	Oil-Seed
Sunflower	Oil, Food	Helicanthus	Composite	Oil-Seed
Sugar Cane	Sugar	Saccarum	Grass	Sugaj
Tobacco	Smoking, Chewing, Medicine, Pesticides	Nicotania tabacum	Nightshad	Special

Lab #7 *(cont.)*

Microsoft Access **Section**

Procedure:

1. Begin this activity by explaining to your students the important role that agriculture plays in our society. United States agriculture is the most advanced in the world. This often-overlooked aspect of our nation's economy is responsible for feeding millions of people around the world by developing and utilizing advanced techniques for producing food. All U.S. citizens should appreciate the food and fiber system that provides them with the highest standard of living on the planet. One of science's most important topics is the role that biotechnology plays in supporting our nation's agriculture. Biotechnology is the use of living organisms to perform a task or produce a product. Today's modern agriculture encompasses many different biotechnologies, including plant science, genetic engineering, beneficial insects, and cultured bacteria. Explain to your class that they will create a database that catalogs thirty-two important crops grown in the United States that support our powerful economy. Students will then use their databases to answer a series of questions that pertain to agriculture.

2. Instruct your students to open new blank database documents, give them the file name (*AGDB*), then click the **Create** button. They should be in the database window where they should create new tables for their information. Instruct your students to click the **New** button, select the **Datasheet** view, and then click the **OK** button. They should now be looking at a blank table that resembles a spreadsheet. Your students should look along the top row at the labels that show the different fields. Remind them that a field is a category under which information will be stored. Instruct your class to click in the cell that is labeled **Field 1**, double-click to highlight the field name, change the first column to (*Common Name*), and press the **Enter** key.

3. Students should adjust the column width in order to see the new label. This is done in a similar manner to increasing column width in a spreadsheet. Instruct your students to bring their cursors up to the line between the **Common Name** field and **Field 2**. When their cursors change to a line with two arrows pointing outward, they should click and hold the mouse button as they drag to the right until the entire label is visible. Instruct your class to adjust the column width for each field. Now they are ready to change the label for **Field 2** to (*Use*). The next three fields to be created should be (*Scientific Name*), (*Family*), and (*Agronomic Classification*).

4. Once your class has labeled all of the fields, explain to them that they will fill in the first record together. Tell them the first crop they should use is wheat. (Remind them that they do not have to enter information into a database alphabetically because it can be sorted later.) Instruct them to type the word (*wheat*) into the first cell below the **Common Name** field. Then they should press the **Tab** key on their keyboards to move them to the next field. The main use of wheat is to make flour, so instruct them to type the word (*flour*) into the **Use** field and then press the **Tab** key.

Lab #7 *(cont.)*

5. The next field requires the scientific name for the crop. Ask your class if they know why it is important for plants to have scientific names. The answer is that scientific names provide a universal way for plants to be identified. Researchers all over the world use scientific names to identify plants. The common names are often different in each country, which makes it difficult to identify specific plants. The scientific name for a plant contains its genus and species name. Instruct students to enter (*Triticum vulgare*) in this field.

6. After your students have entered the scientific name for wheat, they should move to the next field and enter the **Family Classification**. Knowing the family a crop belongs to is important because it identifies how crops are related to one another. This can be significant information because the same insects or diseases might affect plants that are in the same family. Therefore, controlling these problems may be similar for a whole family of crops. Students should enter (*grass*) in the **Family** field. The **Agronomic Classification** field identifies how a crop is used in our society, and how it relates to our nation's economy. Some crops are grown for industrial uses, while others are primarily for feed. This classification helps track the potential market for specific crops. The students' first record is completed and should resemble the one shown in Figure 3.

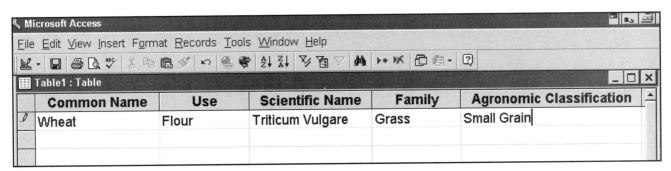

Figure 3. First completed record for the Agricultural Crops database

7. Students can now enter information from the Data Sheet for this lab into their databases. After your students have completed ten complete records, instruct them to save their documents by going to the **FILE** menu and selecting *Save As*. Have them name their tables (*agtable*). A message window will appear that asks if you want to **Create a Primary Key.** A primary key assigns a number for each record. Instruct your students to click the **Yes** button. Explain that they will be able to complete their databases after you have demonstrated some additional database functions.

8. One of the advantages of storing information in a computer database is the ability to sort it. The sorting function allows you to arrange information in a specific way. Explain to your students that they should use the **Sort** function to arrange their databases alphabetically. To do this, they must decide by which field they want to sort. In this case, they will arrange their databases alphabetically by the **Common Name** field.

Lab #7 *(cont.)*

9. Instruct your class to click into the **Common Name** field, then go to the **RECORDS** menu and select *Sort*. Then they can choose either **Sort Ascending** or **Sort Descending**. Sorting a field in ascending order will arrange items from A to Z or 1 to 10. Sorting fields in descending order will arrange items from Z to A or 10 to 1. Instruct your class to choose **Sort Ascending**. Their database tables should now be arranged alphabetically.

10. Another important database function your class will use is the **Search**, or **Filter** function. This allows students to search through their databases for specific information. Explain to your class that they should perform a search for all of the crops that are used for silage. Tell them that silage is chopped corn that is packed in silos or bunkers where it ferments and becomes preserved. The silage is then used as feed for cattle. Instruct them to go to the **RECORDS** menu, select *Filter*, and then choose **Filter by Form**. Your class should be looking at one record containing all blank fields. Instruct them to click in the **Use** field, and type (*silage*). Next, they should go to the **FILTER** menu and select *Apply Filter/Sort*. All of the crops that are used for silage should now be displayed.

11. Explain to your students that to a printout of their results is often referred to as a report, and can be easily generated by using the **New Object** button located on the toolbar (see Figure 4). To create a printed report of their search they should click the small arrow to the right of the **New Object** button.

New Object Icon

Figure 4. The location of the new object button on the *Microsoft Access* toolbar.

12. From the dialog menu, your students should choose **Report**. They will be asked if they want to save the changes to the table in order to create a new object. They should select Yes. Now they can use the **Report Window** to create their reports. Instruct them to choose **Report Wizard** and click **Next**. Here they should choose the fields they want displayed in their reports. To display all of their fields in the report, they should click the double arrow icon to select all of the fields in the record, and then click **Next**.

13. The next window of the **Report Wizard** asks if they want to set grouping levels. Instruct your students to leave this unchanged and move to the next window. Instruct your students to click the small arrow next to the blank **Sort** box window and choose **Common Name**. This will sort their report alphabetically by the **Common Name** field.

Lab #7 *(cont.)*

14. The next window asks how they want to display their fields in the report. Instruct your students to select **Tabular** and click the **Next** button. At the next window, have students choose the style in which they would like to display their report. The final window asks them to name the report. In this example, instruct your class to name the report (*Silage*) and click the **Finish** button. Their report should now be displayed and ready for printing.

15. Instruct students to close the report and return to their tables. To display all of the records of their database once again, they should click the icon at the top of the screen that resembles a funnel, located to the left of the binoculars icon. This button will remove the filter. Explain to your class that closing their tables and clicking the **Report** tab in the database window (see Figure 5) will retrieve their reports. They can also reopen their tables by clicking the **Table** tab.

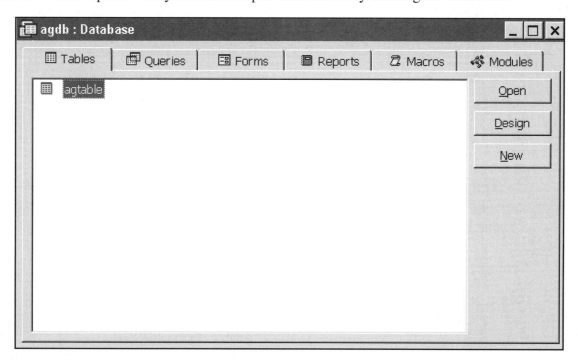

Figure 5. The database window for *Microsoft Access*

16. Your students should now continue to fill in the records for their database until it is complete. Once they have completed entering all of the information into their database, students can perform the functions and answer the questions on the Agricultural Database Work Sheet.

This completes the activity.

Lab #7 *(cont.)*

Microsoft Access Template for Lab #7

ID	Common Name	Use	Scientific Name	Family	Agronomic Classification
1	Wheat	Flour	Triticum vulgare	Grass	Small Grain
2	Oats	Feed, Food Grain	Avena sativa	Grass	Small Grain
3	Barley	Feed, Malt	Hordeum vulgare	Grass	Small Grain
4	Rye	Feed, Flour, Pasture, Cover	Secale cereale	Grass	Small Garin
5	Rice	Food Grain	Oryza sativa	Grass	Small Grain
6	Corn	Feed, Silage, Food Grain, Oil, Sugar, Starch, Industry	Zea mays	Grass	Grain, Oil Seed
7	Soy Beans	Feed, Food, Oil	Glycine max	Legume	Oil-Seed
8	Sorghum	Feed, Silage	Sorghum vulgare	Grass	Grain
9	Cotton	Textiles, Oil	Gossypium hirsutum	Mallow	Fiber, Oil-Seed
10	Alfalfa	Hay, Pasture, Cover	Medicago sativa	Legume	Forage
11	Sweet Clover	Pasture, Cover	Melilotus alba	Legume	Forage
12	Red Clover	Hay, Pasture, Cover	Trifolium pratense	Legume	Forage
13	White Clover	Hay, Pasture, Silage, Cover	Trifolium repens	Legume	Forage
14	Trefoil	Hay, pasture, Cover	Lotus tenius	Legume	Forage
15	Timothy	Hay, Pasture, Cver	Phleum pratense	Grass	Forage
16	Orchard Grass	Hay, Silage, Pasture	Dactylis glomerata	Grass	Forage
17	Smooth Brome Grass	Hay, Silage, Pasture	Bromus inermus	Grass	Forage
18	Kentucky Bluegrass	Turf, Pasture	Poa pratensis	Grass	Forage
19	Bermuda Grass	Turf, Pasture	Cynodon dactylon	Grass	Forage
20	Tall Fescue	Hay, Pasture	Festuca elatior	Grass	Forage
21	Annual Lespedeza	Hay, Pasture, Cover	Lespedeza striata	Legume	Forage
22	Sudan Grass	Hay, Silage, Pasture	Sorghum vulgare	Grass	Forage
23	Foxtail Millet	Hay	Setaria italica	Grass	Forage
24	Buckwheat	Flour	Fagopyrum esculentu	Buckwheat	Grain
25	Canola	Oil, Industry	Brassica napus	Mustard	Oil-Seed
26	Dry Beans	Food, Feed	Phaseolus vulgaris	Legume	Oil-Seed
27	Flax	Oil, Linen, Straw	Linum usitatissium	Flax	Oil and Fiber
28	Peanuts	Oil, Food	Arachis hypogaea	Legume	Root and Sugar
29	Sugar Beets	Sugar, Feed	Beta vulgaris	Goosefoot	Oil-Seed
30	Sunflower	Oil, Food	Helicanthus annuuss	Composite	Oil-Seed
31	Sugar Cane	Sugar	Saccarum officinarum	Grass	Sugar
32	Tobacco	Smoking, Chewing, Medicine, Pesticides	Nicotania tabacum	Nightshade	Special

Lab #8 Intermediate LOGO Programming: The Obstacle Course

Purpose:

Students use the *LOGO* programming language to create simple obstacle courses in which to successfully guide their "turtles." The use of *LOGO* helps students to understand the way computer languages and codes are used to program computers. Although *LOGO* is a simple computer language, it applies the same techniques used to program complex computer applications, thus making this an excellent introductory lesson to computer programming. Some knowledge of *LOGO* programming is helpful, but not essential for the successful implementation of this activity.

Learning Objectives:

At the end of this lesson, each student will be able to:

- utilize the following *LOGO* command codes: fd, bk, rt, lt, cs, home, pu, pd, seth, setpc, and setxy.

- explain how the coordinate system is used in the *LOGO* graphics screen.

- create, name, and save a procedure.

- successfully run a procedure.

- explain how sub procedures can be grouped together to form larger procedures.

- write a procedure, using sub procedures, that will create a maze.

- successfully navigate the "turtle" through a maze using *LOGO* commands.

Materials:

- *LOGO* application program. (There are many different versions of *LOGO* available, and this activity should work well with all of them. This activity was written for use with *Berkeley LOGO*, which is a free version available to download via the Internet. If you are interested in obtaining a free copy of *Berkeley LOGO*, use an Internet search engine to locate a Web site from which it can be downloaded.)

- *LOGO* Commands hand out on page 88 for each student

Lab #8 *(cont.)*

LOGO Commands

fd 10 = Moves the turtle forward 10 steps

bk 10 = Moves the turtle backwards 10 steps

rt 90 = Turns the turtle 90 degrees to the right

lt 90 = Turns the turtle 90 degrees to the left

cs = Clears the screen (clear screen)

pd = Puts the turtle's pen down

pu = Puts the turtle's pen up

seth 180 = Sets the turtle's heading to 180 degrees

setxy 40-40 = Moves the turtle's location to coordinates 40-40

home = Moves the turtle to the home position (center of the screen)

repeat 4 [fd 10 rt 90] = Moves the turtle forward 10 steps and right 90 degrees, 4 times

setpc 2 = Turns pen color to green

setbg 1 = Turns background color to blue

color codes: 0 = black, **1** = blue, **2** = green, **3** = light blue, **4** = red, **5** = pink, **6** = yellow, **7** = white

Obstacle Course Procedures

to course1	to course2	to course3	to course4
pu	pu	pu	pu
setxy 220 -100	setxy -150 75	setxy 120 -50	setxy -50 20
seth 0	seth 180	seth 0	seth 180
pd	pd	pd	pd
fd 200	fd 175	fd 100	fd 50
lt 90	lt 90	lt 90	lt 90
fd 400	fd 325	fd 200	fd 125
lt 90	lt 90	lt 90	lt 90
fd 200	fd 175	fd 100	fd 50
pu	pu	pu	pu
end	end	end	end

Lab #8 *(cont.)*

Procedure:

1. To begin this activity, summarize for your students a short history of the *LOGO* programming language. *LOGO* is a simple computer programming language that was developed by a group of computer scientists working at the Massachusetts Institute of Technology. The scientists at MIT developed *LOGO* to control small robots, called turtles, using a simple computer language. Written commands give the turtle instructions to perform specific tasks. Although *LOGO* was originally designed for use with robots, it can be used to manipulate a simulated turtle on a graphics screen.

2. Instruct your students to open the *LOGO* program, and explain to them that *LOGO* utilizes two screens, the first of which is called the **Procedures** window. This window is where the command codes are typed for controlling the turtle. The second window is called the **Graphics** window and is where the turtle moves around the screen. Instruct your students to arrange their screens so they are both completely visible. This is accomplished by clicking the title bar of a window and dragging to relocate it.

3. Next, explain to your students that the object at the center of the graphics screen is the turtle. This is the robot that they will manipulate with the *LOGO* programming code. Also explain to them that they are looking at the turtle from above. Therefore, if the turtle were to move forward, it would appear to be moving upwards on their screen. Students should begin to move the turtle by typing some of the simple command codes into the **Procedures** window. Instruct them to type (*fd 100*) into the **Procedures** window. Students should press the **Return** or **Enter** key on their keyboards to carry out this command. Ask your class what happened to the turtle. They should notice that it moved forward one hundred steps and also drew a line. Explain to them that the turtle has a pen attached to it and can draw a line whenever it moves. Next, your students should type (*bk 100*). Remind them that all of the *LOGO* commands will be carried out only when the **Return** or **Enter** key has been pressed. The turtle should now have moved backward 100 steps.

4. The next two commands involve turning the turtle right or left. Explain to your students that the turtle turns with respect to the degrees of a circle. Instruct your class to type the command (*rt 90*). Ask your class what happened. They should notice that the turtle rotated on its axis ninety degrees to the right. Next, instruct your class to type the command (*lt 90*). This will turn the turtle ninety degrees to the left. The (seth) command, which is the Set Heading command, will also program a turtle's direction. For example, if your students want their turtle to turn in a 45-degree direction, they should type the command (*seth 45*).

Lab #8 *(cont.)*

5. Now that your class knows some simple *LOGO* codes, they should program the turtle to draw a square. To do this, they should type the following code into the **Procedures** window:

fd 100

rt 90

fd 100

rt 90

fd 100

rt 90

fd 100

rt 90

The turtle should have drawn a square, and their screens should resemble the one in Figure 1.

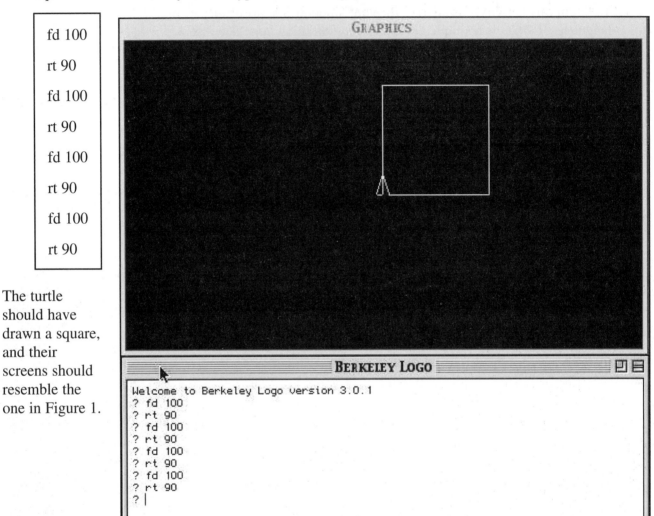

Figure 1. *LOGO* commands for drawing a square

6. Next, instruct your students to type the command (*cs*) to clear their screen. Now instruct your students to type (*pu*). Then have them command the turtle to draw a square again. Your students should notice immediately that the turtle is no longer drawing a line. This is because the (*pu*) command instructs the turtle to pick its pen up, preventing it from drawing a line. Have your class type the command (*pd*), which instructs the turtle to put its pen down.

Lab #8 *(cont.)*

7. Now that your students have learned the basic commands for controlling a turtle, they are going to learn some advanced commands that will help them create an obstacle course for the turtle to navigate. Explain that the turtle can also move around the screen using coordinates. All computer screens utilize the coordinate system to identify exact locations on the screen. This is the same method the computer mouse uses to select objects on a screen, which helps to make modern computers so easy to use. This is also known as graphical interfacing. The turtle's graphic screen consists of a grid pattern of x-axis and y-axis coordinates. The center of the graphics screen, also known as the home position, has an x coordinate of 0 and a y coordinate of 0. Figure 2 illustrates the way the screen is laid out using coordinates.

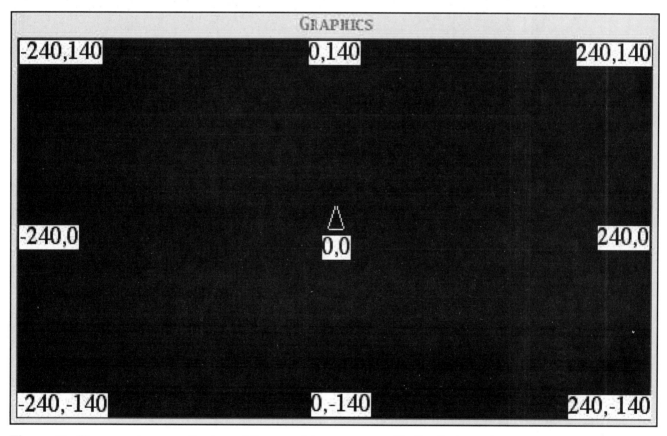

Figure 2. The x and y coordinates of the graphics screen, with the first number representing the x-axis

8. By using the (*setxy*) command, your students can move the turtle to an exact location on their screens. Have them type the command (*setxy 120 120*). Their turtle should now be located in the upper-right of their screen at coordinates x 120, and y 120. Next, instruct your students to clear their screens using the (*cs*) command, and move their turtle to coordinates -120, -120. The turtle should now be located in the bottom-left portion of the screen.

Lab #8 *(cont.)*

9. Explain to your students that so far they have been controlling the turtle using individual commands, but it is also possible to put together commands to instruct the turtle to perform many functions at once. This is called a *procedure*. A procedure is much like a computer program that provides many lines of instructions to perform complex tasks. Have your students write a procedure to draw an object on the screen. Explain to them that all procedures begin with the (to) command, and all procedures must also be named. When naming a procedure there can be no spaces between letters. Instruct your students to type the following procedure:

```
to square

cs

fd 100

rt 90

fd 100

rt 90

fd 100

rt 90

fd 100

rt 90

end
```

10. Notice that all procedures must end with the (*end*) command. Once the procedure is written, a message will appear that reads **square defined**. This tells your students that the procedure is stored in memory. To run a procedure, they should type the name, in this example (*square*), and the turtle should draw a square instantaneously in the graphics screen.

11. Next, your students should create four new procedures. Distribute copies of the *LOGO* Commands hand out, which contains the procedures that they should enter. The procedures are also listed on the next page for your reference.

Lab #8 *(cont.)*

to course1	to course2	to course3	to course4
pu	pu	pu	pu
setxy 220 -100	setxy -150 75	setxy 120 -50	setxy -50 20
seth 0	seth 180	seth 0	seth 180
pd	pd	pd	pd
fd 200	fd 175	fd 100	fd 50
lt 90	lt 90	lt 90	lt 90
fd 400	fd 325	fd 200	fd 125
lt 90	lt 90	lt 90	lt 90
fd 200	fd 175	fd 100	fd 50
pu	pu	pu	pu
end	end	end	end

12. Once your students have created their four new procedures, they should test them to make sure they all work. Figure 3 shows how all four procedures, if programmed properly, should look on the graphics screen. Once you have checked all of your students' procedures, instruct them to clear their screens.

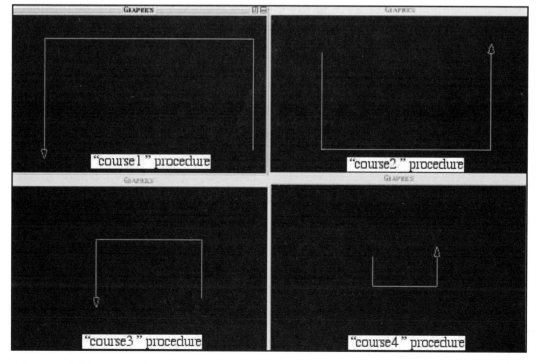

Figure 3. All four of the correctly programmed procedures

                   #2709 Computer Projects for Middle Schools

Lab #8 *(cont.)*

13. Next, explain to your class that it is possible to combine procedures together to make one complex procedure. In this example, your students should combine the four course procedures they have just programmed to create a new procedure called (*obcourse*). The four original procedures now are referred to as *sub-procedures*. The technique of using sub-procedures in computer programming is common and is used to create large, complex programs. Often different programmers work on separate sub-procedures that are later combined to create a complete program. This new procedure that will create an obstacle course for their turtles to navigate. Students should create the following new procedure:

```
to obcourse

course1

course2

course3

course4

end
```

14. Point out to your students how the four previous procedures have been added together to create a new procedure. Once they have created the new procedure, they should clear their screens and then run the procedure by typing (*obcourse*). Point out to them how the four procedures have now been added together to create the obstacle course. Their screens should resemble the one in Figure 4.

Lab #8 *(cont.)*

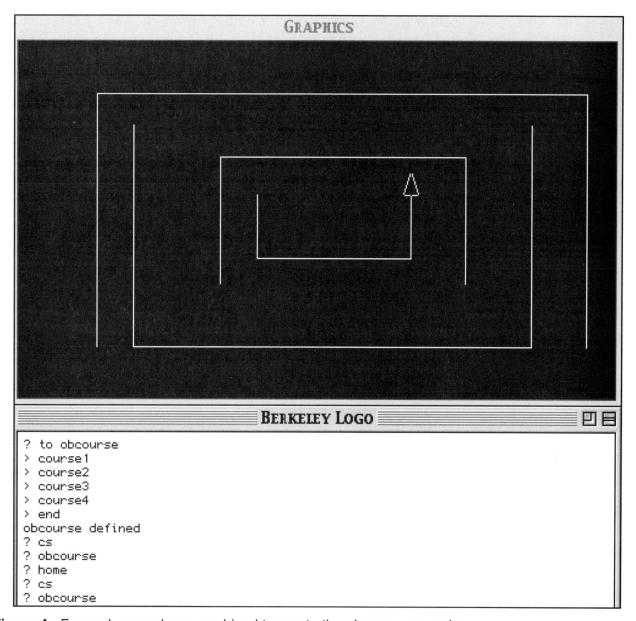

Figure 4. Four sub procedures combined to create the obcourse procedure

15. Instruct your students to type the (*home*) command, which will put the turtle in the center of the obstacle course. Explain to them that they should now put the turtle's pen down. Then they should alter the color of the line drawn by the pen. The (*setpc*) command is the pen color command, where each color is given a code. The color codes are shown on the *LOGO* Commands hand out. Explain to your students that in this example they should set the pen color to red by typing the command (*setpc 4*). Your students can then successfully navigate the turtle out of the maze by typing correct commands. Remind them that they must not cross any of the lines.

This completes the activity.

Lab #8 (cont.)

Notes:

_____

_____

_____

_____

_____

_____

_____

_____

_____

_____

_____

_____

_____

_____

_____

_____

_____

_____

_____

_____

_____

_____

Lab #9 Advanced Computer-Assisted Drawing: Latitude and Longitude

Purpose:

Students are introduced to the technical applications of computer-assisted drawing as they create accurate maps of the world that depict major lines of latitude and longitude, along with appropriate labels. Cartography and the creation of computer-generated maps is one of the most important applications of today's computer technology, allowing for the production of the most accurate maps to date.

Learning Objectives:

At the end of this lesson, each student will be able to:

- open a new drawing document.

- change the viewing size and page orientation of a drawing.

- insert and lock a graphic into a drawing.

- use the rulers and line tool in a drawing.

- increase and decrease line thickness.

- label objects in a drawing.

- change a label's font size, style, and color in a drawing.

- move an object in a drawing.

- group objects in a drawing.

- save and name a new drawing document.

- identify and label the major lines of latitude and longitude on the earth.

Materials:

- *AppleWorks* (*ClarisWorks*) or *Microsoft Word* (A computer drawing application is needed for this laboratory; however, a complex CAD application program is not required. Multi-use application programs are excellent for this activity due to their ease of use and wide availability.)

- Latitude and Longitude hand out from the following page

- (*worldmap.jpg*) JPEG file from the CD-ROM

Lab #9 *(cont.)*

Latitude and Longitude

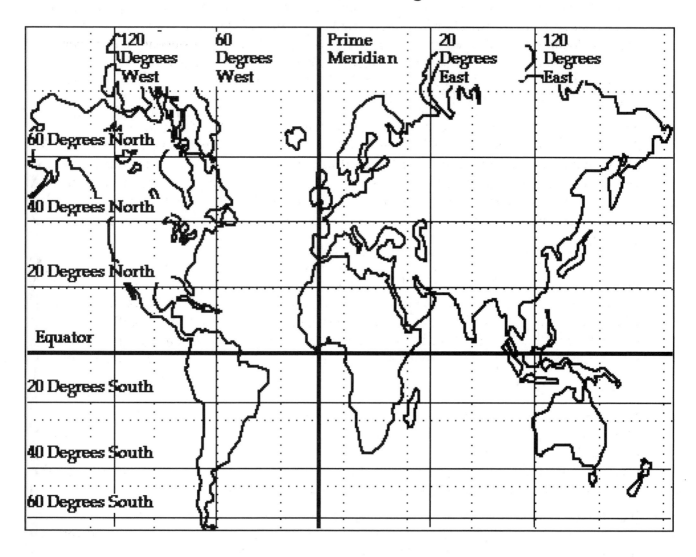

Lab #9 *(cont.)*

Procedure:

1. Begin this activity by explaining to your students the important role that computer generated maps play in our society. If your class is using *AppleWorks* (*ClarisWorks*), direct students to open new drawing documents on their computers. If using *Microsoft Word*, direct students to open new documents and make sure the drawing toolbar is displayed. Students should choose the **Page View** or **Page Layout view** to clearly see the margins of the page. It is also important to have the rulers showing on the page with the units set to inches.

2. Next, have your students reduce the viewing size of their documents. If they are using *AppleWorks* (*ClarisWorks*) with a Macintosh, a 67% view is perfect for this project. A 48% view allows you to see the entire page in *Microsoft Word*. Reducing the viewing size of their pages will allow students to see more of the map, and will also make it easier for them to add to their drawings. Now students should change the orientation of their pages. The **Landscape** (or sideways) orientation creates a more usable drawing space for producing an accurate world map. This option can be found in *Page Setup* from the **FILE** menu.

3. After all of the formatting for their drawing document has been set, your students should be ready to insert a graphic into their drawings. Inserting a line map of the earth will increase the accuracy of their maps, while also saving them time. In *Microsoft Word*, go to the **INSERT** menu, select *Picture*, and choose **From File**. Insert the (*worldmap.jpg*) graphic. If using *AppleWorks* (*ClarisWorks*), go to the **FILE** menu, select *Insert*, and insert the (*worldmap.jpg*) graphic and have it float over the text. If inserted as text, the graphic is much more difficult to resize and move around the page. This is accomplished by choosing the Pointer tool before inserting the graphic. Once the map has been inserted into their drawings, each student should click and drag the map's anchor points, stretching them so that the map fits on an entire page. Each corner anchor point should be aligned with the corners of the page margins to allow for maximum use of one printable page. If your class is using *AppleWorks* (*ClarisWorks*), you may wish to have students lock the graphic into place so that it cannot be moved during the rest of the activity. To do this, they should go to the **ARRANGE** menu and choose **Lock**.

4. In order to make it easier for your students to place the lines of latitude in the correct location on their map, it is useful to use a coordinate system. Students should use the horizontal and vertical ruler measurements as a coordinate guide. The horizontal ruler should act as the x-coordinate and the vertical ruler measurement as the y-coordinate. This will allow you to guide your students to the exact starting locations on their page for each line. The first and most widely known latitudinal line is the equator. The equator divides our globe in half. However, on a flat representation of the earth like in the (*worldmap*) graphic, the equator is not located at the center of the page. Figure 1 shows the location of the equator when using the vertical ruler (x-coordinate) at the five-inch mark.

Lab #9 *(cont.)*

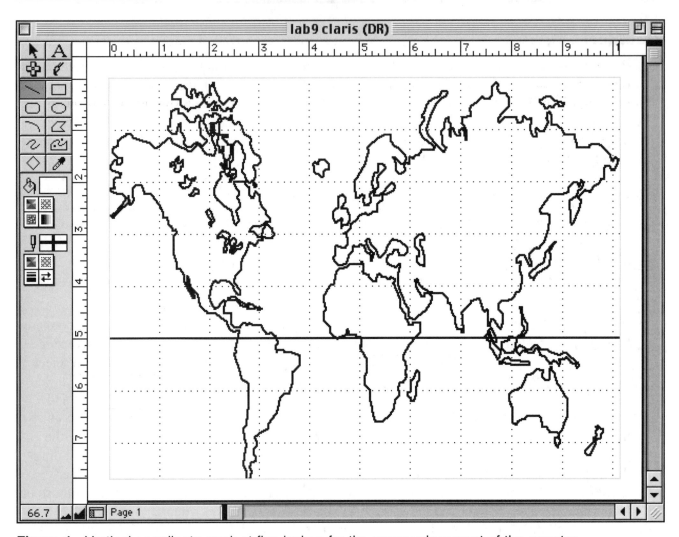

Figure 1. Vertical coordinate mark at five inches for the proper placement of the equator

5. The use of different drawing application programs will require different coordinate placement of the major lines of latitude and longitude on the page. To help you locate the position of each specific line, see Figure 2, which shows a completed map using *AppleWorks* (*ClarisWorks*) on a Macintosh. Notice the geographic locations where the lines cross the continents. Also notice how the lines of latitude are not evenly spaced due to the distortion of the earth created by a Mercator map projection. The Latitude and Longitude hand out also shows the proper placement of the latitude and longitude lines. You may wish to try to produce your own complete map drawing by yourself first, using the specific drawing application you have available for your students. This will help you predetermine the starting x and y coordinates of each line, and which measurement best fits your drawing application's page margins. Table 1 and Figure 2 show the approximate coordinates and the completed map for *AppleWorks* (*ClarisWorks*). Table 2 and Figure 3 show the approximate coordinates and the completed map for *Microsoft Word*.

Lab #9 *(cont.)*

Lines of Latitude	Lines of Longitude
0 Degrees North: Y-coordinate = 5"	0 Degrees: X-coordinate = 4 5/8"
20 Degrees North: Y-coordinate = 4"	60 Degrees East: X-coordinate = 6 3/8"
40 Degrees North: Y-coordinate = 3"	120 Degrees East: X-coordinate = 8"
60 Degrees North: Y-coordinate = 2"	60 Degrees West: X-coordinate = 3"
20 Degrees South: Y-coordinate = 5 3/4"	120 Degrees West: X-coordinate = 1 3/8"
40 Degrees South: Y-coordinate = 6 3/4"	
60 Degrees South: Y-coordinate = 7 1/2"	

Table 1: Latitude and longitude line coordinates for an *AppleWorks* (*ClarisWorks*) drawing document

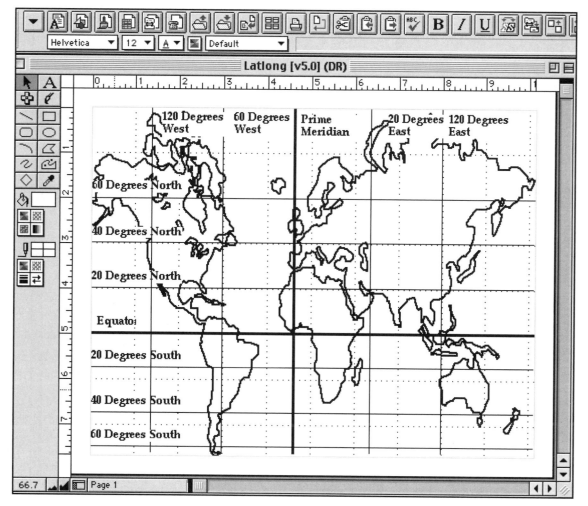

Figure 2. Completed latitude and longitude map using *AppleWorks* (*ClarisWorks*).

Lab #9 *(cont.)*

Lines of Latitude	Lines of Longitude
0 Degrees North: Y-coordinate = 5"	0 Degrees: X-coordinate = 4⅝"
20 Degrees North: Y-coordinate = 4"	60 Degrees East: X-coordinate = 6⅜"
40 Degrees North: Y-coordinate = 3¼"	120 Degrees East: X-coordinate = 8"
60 Degrees North: Y-coordinate = 2"	60 Degrees West: X-coordinate = 3"
20 Degrees South: Y-coordinate = 5¾"	120 Degrees West: X-coordinate = 1⅜"
40 Degrees South: Y-coordinate = 6¾"	
60 Degrees South: Y-coordinate = 7½"	

Table 2: Approximate longitude and longitude line coordinates for drawing with *Microsoft Word*

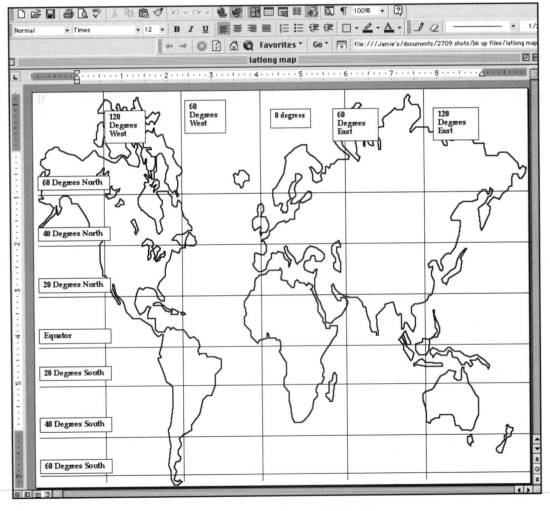

Figure 3. Completed latitude longitude map using *Microsoft Word*

Lab #9 *(cont.)*

6. After you have explained to your students how to use the coordinate system, they should choose the **Line** tool on their toolbars, and you should begin to provide them with the latitude coordinates. Students should start with the equator and work northward by drawing the lines of latitude in twenty-degree increments. When all of the students have successfully drawn the northern latitude lines, they should begin the southern latitude lines.

7. Students should select the equator line and increase its thickness so it stands out from the other lines of latitude. Then they will need to properly label their latitude lines. Direct them to use the **Text** tool in *AppleWorks* (*ClarisWorks*) or the **Text Box** tool in *Microsoft Word*. Students should place each label on top of its latitude line along the left margin using a font size of at least 14-point. Encourage your students to choose a unique font for their labels, but make sure the font they use is clearly readable.

8. Once the latitude lines are correctly labeled, your students should begin adding the lines of longitude. The first line of longitude to be drawn should be the Greenwich, or Prime Meridian, representing zero degrees longitude. After it has been drawn, students should add the lines of East longitude. Because of the limited size of the map, the lines of longitude should be drawn every sixty degrees. After they have completed the East longitude, they should add the lines of West longitude. Students should then label their lines of longitude and increase the Prime Meridian line thickness.

9. When your class has completed their maps, they can use them to locate the latitude and longitude of some specific areas on Earth. For example, ask them to find what the approximate latitude and longitude are for China, Washington State, and Argentina. Also ask your students to explain how computers make it easier to draw more accurate maps. You may wish to have your students print out copies of their maps, making sure they add their name somewhere on it before printing. There are many extensions that can be applied to this activity, depending on the time and subject matter that students might be studying in other classes. This activity might provide a good way to align your curriculum with other disciplines, or show how computer technology can be used in many subject areas.

This completes the activity.

Lab #9 *(cont.)*

Notes:

_____

_____

_____

_____

_____

_____

_____

_____

_____

_____

_____

_____

_____

_____

_____

_____

_____

_____

_____

_____

_____

_____

_____

Lab #10 Advanced Spreadsheets: Household Electrical Use

Note: Because of the differences that exist in creating a spreadsheet in *AppleWorks* (*ClarisWorks*) and *Microsoft Excel*, this lesson is divided into two separate sections. The first section deals with using *AppleWorks* (*ClarisWorks*); and the second section, beginning on page 114, focuses on *Microsoft Excel*.

Purpose:

Students are introduced to the use of spreadsheet formulas by creating spreadsheets that track the electrical usage of a common household. Spreadsheet formulas are used to program specific cells to automatically perform mathematical calculations.

Learning Objectives:

At the end of this lesson, each student will be able to:

- format a spreadsheet to track electrical use.

- create spreadsheet formulas within a cell.

- insert preprogrammed formulas into a cell.

- use cell formulas to calculate watt-hours.

- use cell formulas to calculate kilowatt-hours.

- use cell formulas to calculate the cost of electrical use.

- format a cell to display numbers as currency.

Materials:

- *AppleWorks* (*ClarisWorks*) or *Microsoft Excel* spreadsheet application

- Data Sheet from page 106

- (*Elecuse.cws*) *AppleWorks* (*ClarisWorks*) template or (*Elecuse.xls*) *Microsoft Excel* template from the CD-ROM (optional)

(If using the template file, begin the lesson with step 6.)

Lab #10 *(cont.)*

Data Sheet

Wattage requirements and average daily use for common appliances

Appliance	Hours/Day Used	Wattage
TV (19-inch color)	5	60
Refrigerator	12	490
Incandescent Light	8	75
Electric Clock	24	12
Clock Radio	24	10
Stereo	4	15
Computer	3	80
Dishwasher	1	1500
Washing Machine	1	450
Dryer	1	250

Lab #10 *(cont.)*

AppleWorks (*ClarisWorks*) **Spreadsheet Section**

Procedure:

1. Begin this activity by explaining to your students that spreadsheet applications are not only used for creating charts and graphs but also used as calculators to manipulate numerical data. Cells in a spreadsheet can be programmed to automatically perform mathematical calculations. This is how many businesses track inventory and sales. Explain to your class that they are going to create spreadsheets that track common electrical use in a typical house.

2. Instruct your students to open new spreadsheet documents. Direct them to click in cell A1. To begin this exercise, they should create column labels for each type of electrical use data that they will track. The label to be entered in cell A1 is (*Appliance*). After entering this label, students should press the **Tab** key on their keyboards to move to cell B1. The next label should read (*hours/days used*). The third label entered into cell C1 should be (*wattage*), and the fourth label for column D should be (*watt-hours*). The label in cell E1 should be (*kilowatt-hours*), and the last label, located in cell F1, should be (*cost*). Remind students to press the **Tab** key after each entry. Once your students have entered all of their column labels, instruct them to change the font style to bold for each label and center the data in the cell. Your students' spreadsheets should now resemble Figure 1.

	A	B	C	D	E	F
1	Appliance	Hours/Day Used	Wattage	Watt Hours	Kilowatt Hours	Cost
2						
3						

Figure 1. Electrical use spreadsheet column labels

3. The appliances listed in the data sheet for this lab are contained in a typical house. Distribute a copy of the data sheet to each of your students. Instruct them to enter the names of the appliances into column A, beginning with cell A2 and ending with cell A11.

4. The data sheet also contains the average number hours each appliance is used on a normal day. Instruct your class to enter this information into column B of their spreadsheets.

Lab #10 *(cont.)*

5. Your students are now ready to enter the amount of wattage these appliances consume when they are in use. Instruct your students to fill the required wattage into the correct cells in column C. When your class has entered all of their wattage requirements, their spreadsheets should resemble the one in Figure 2.

	A	B	C	D	E	F
1	**Appliance**	**Hours/Day Used**	**Wattage**	**Watt Hours**	**Kilowatt Hours**	**Cost**
2	TV 19 inch color	5	60			
3	refrigerator	12	490			
4	incandescent light	8	75			
5	electric clock	24	12			
6	clock radio	24	10			
7	stereo	4	15			
8	computer	3	80			
9	dishwasher	1	1500			
10	washing machine	1	450			
11	dryer	1	250			
12						

Figure 2. Completed spreadsheet with hours/day used and wattage requirements for electrical use

6. Explain to your students that column D, Watt Hours, is the manner in which the electric company measures electrical use. It is calculated by multiplying the wattage consumed by the hours a day the appliance is being used. For example, if a sixty-watt light bulb were used for two hours, then its total consumption would be 120 watt-hours. Explain to them that they are going to enter a formula into cell D2 that will automatically calculate watt-hours. A cell formula is a mathematical expression that uses data from other cells to calculate specific information. Explain to your class that they are going to create a cell formula that will multiply the number of hours a refrigerator is used by its wattage requirement.

7. Instruct your students to click in cell D2 and type the formula (=B2*C2). Explain to your class that all cell formulas begin with the "=" sign. This instructs the spreadsheet that a formula is being programmed into a cell. Also point out that a formula uses cell addresses in the mathematical expression. The sign for multiplication in a spreadsheet is the "*" symbol, or asterisk. Once students have entered the formula into the cell, they should press the **Return** key on their keyboards. Cell D2 will display the product of multiplying the data in cell B2 by the data in cell C2—300 watt-hours. Explain to your class that the contents of cell D2 will automatically change if the numbers in cells B2 or C2 are changed. For example, have your students change the amount of hours the television is used from five to ten and press the **Return** key. Students should notice how the number in the watt-hours column also changed. This is one of the advantages of using spreadsheet formulas. You can constantly change the numbers in specific cells, and the formulas will still be applied. This is how businesses use spreadsheets to track inventory or automatically apply sales tax.

Lab #10 *(cont.)*

8. Now ask your students what formula should be used to automatically calculate watt-hours for the refrigerator. Instruct them to enter the formula (*=B3*C3*) into cell D3. Once they understand the watt-hour formula concept, instruct them to complete the formulas for the rest of column D. When they are finished, their spreadsheets should resemble the one in Figure 3.

D11	▼ fx ✕ ✓	=B11*C11			
	A	**B**	**C**	**D**	**E**	**F**
1	**Appliance**	**Hours/Day Used**	**Wattage**	**Watt Hours**	**Kilowatt Hours**	**Cost**
2	TV 19 inch color	5	60	300		
3	refrigerator	12	490	5880		
4	incandescent light	8	75	600		
5	electric clock	24	12	288		
6	clock radio	24	10	240		
7	stereo	4	15	60		
8	computer	3	80	240		
9	dishwasher	1	1500	1500		
10	washing machine	1	450	450		
11	dryer	1	250	250		
12						

Figure 3. Watt-hours automatically calculated by cell formulas in column D

9. Next, instruct your students to enter formulas into column E that will automatically calculate kilowatt-hours. Ask your students if they know what a kilowatt-hour is. (A kilowatt-hour equals one thousand watt-hours, and is used by the electric companies to measure electrical usage.) Electricity is consumed at such a high rate that watt-hours are too small of a measurement, so kilowatt-hours are used instead. Ask students which formula should be entered in cell E2 to calculate the kilowatt-hours used by the TV in one day. Explain that they must divide the total amount of watts from cell D2 by one thousand (*=D2/1000*). Also point out that the symbol for division used in a spreadsheet formula is the "/" symbol, or backslash. They should enter the formula into cell D2 and press the **Return** key. The answer displayed in cell E2 of their spreadsheets should be (*0.3*). Once your students understand the kilowatt-hour formula, they should enter the rest of the formulas for column E. When they have completed this task, their spreadsheets should resemble the one in Figure 4.

Lab #10 *(cont.)*

E11	▼	fx	✕	✓	=D11/1000		

	A	**B**	**C**	**D**	**E**	**F**
1	Appliance	Hours/Day Used	Wattage	Watt Hours	Kilowatt Hours	Cost
2	TV 19 inch color	5	60	300	0.3	
3	refrigerator	12	490	5880	5.88	
4	incandescent light	8	75	600	0.6	
5	electric clock	24	12	288	0.288	
6	clock radio	24	10	240	0.24	
7	stereo	4	15	60	0.06	
8	computer	3	80	240	0.24	
9	dishwasher	1	1500	1500	1.5	
10	washing machine	1	450	450	0.45	
11	dryer	1	250	250	0.25	
12						

Figure 4. Completed formulas for kilowatt-hours in column E.

10. The final column of the electrical use spreadsheet deals with the cost of electricity. Explain to your students that the electric company calculates the cost of electricity by the kilowatt-hour. Although electrical costs vary by state and the time of day, for this example your students should use 14 cents as the cost of a kilowatt-hour. Ask your class which formula should be in cell F2, where the cost of the electricity used by the TV is calculated. The answer is (*=E2*.14*). Once this formula is entered, the contents of cell F2 should be (*.042*).

11. The answer will need to be altered to show the value to the nearest cent. To accomplish this, your class should click into cell F2, go to the **FORMAT** menu, and select *Number*. Then they should choose **Currency**, and click the **OK** button. The number in cell F2 should now be displayed in dollars and cents. Instruct your students to complete the cost formulas for the rest of column F. Remind them that they must also display all of the values in that column as currency.

12. Once your students have completed entering all of the formulas and formatting the last column, explain to them that *AppleWorks* (*ClarisWorks*) provides many preprogrammed formulas. Students should click into cell A12, type the label (***Total***), and make it bold. In cell B12 they are going to use a preprogrammed formula that will add all of the data in column B. To accomplish this, your class should choose the **EDIT** menu, and select *Paste Function*. The **Paste Function** window, which contains the preprogrammed functions, will appear.

Lab #10 *(cont.)*

13. Instruct your students to scroll down the list until they see the (**=SUM(number1,number2,...)** function. They should select this function and click **OK**. The formula should now be displayed in the cell window at the top of the spreadsheet. Now students should click in the cell window and drag to highlight all of the data between the parenthesis (see Figure 5).

B12	▼ *fx* ✕ ✓	=SUM(number1,number2,...)			
	A	**B**	**C**	**D**	**E**	**F**
1	**Appliance**	**Hours/Day Used**	**Wattage**	**Watt Hours**	**Kilowatt Hours**	**Cost**
2	TV 19 inch color	5	60	300	0.3	$0.04
3	refrigerator	12	490	5880	5.88	$0.82
4	incandescent light	8	75	600	0.6	$0.08
5	electric clock	24	12	288	0.288	$0.04
6	clock radio	24	10	240	0.24	$0.03
7	stereo	4	15	60	0.06	$0.01
8	computer	3	80	240	0.24	$0.03
9	dishwasher	1	1500	1500	1.5	$0.21
10	washing machine	1	450	450	0.45	$0.06
11	dryer	1	250	250	0.25	$0.04
12	**Total**					
13						

Figure 5. Data highlighted between the parenthesis in the sum function

14. Once your students have highlighted the data between the parenthesis of the sum function, they should click into cell B2, hold down the mouse button, and drag down column B until they reach cell B11. Once they reach cell B11, your students should let go of the mouse button and press the **Return** key on their keyboards. This procedure will automatically program the sum function to add together all of the data in column B from cell B2 to cell B11 and display the answer in cell B12. If done correctly, the answer displayed in cell B12 should be (*83*). If your students make a mistake, instruct them to once again highlight the data between the parenthesis of the sum function, and click and drag over the data in column B that they want added. Remind them to stop at cell B11. Their spreadsheets should now resemble the one in Figure 6.

B12	▼ *fx* ✕ ✓	=SUM(B2..B11)			
	A	**B**	**C**	**D**	**E**	**F**
1	**Appliance**	**Hours/Day Used**	**Wattage**	**Watt Hours**	**Kilowatt Hours**	**Cost**
2	TV 19 inch color	5	60	300	0.3	$0.04
3	refrigerator	12	490	5880	5.88	$0.82
4	incandescent light	8	75	600	0.6	$0.08
5	electric clock	24	12	288	0.288	$0.04
6	clock radio	24	10	240	0.24	$0.03
7	stereo	4	15	60	0.06	$0.01
8	computer	3	80	240	0.24	$0.03
9	dishwasher	1	1500	1500	1.5	$0.21
10	washing machine	1	450	450	0.45	$0.06
11	dryer	1	250	250	0.25	$0.04
12	**Total**	83				
13						

Figure 6. The sum function in cell B12 adding together all of the data in column B

Lab #10 *(cont.)*

15. Once your students have mastered the **Paste Function** command, instruct them to complete their spreadsheets by inserting and programming the sum function below each column. Once they have completed this, they should change the format of the number in cell F12 to currency, and their spreadsheets should resemble the one in Figure 7. They should save this file as (elecuse).

	A	B	C	D	E	F
	Appliance	Hours/Day Used	Wattage	Watt Hours	Kilowatt Hours	Cost
2	TV 19 inch color	5	60	300	0.3	$0.04
3	refrigerator	12	490	5880	5.88	$0.82
4	incandescent light	8	75	600	0.6	$0.08
5	electric clock	24	12	288	0.288	$0.04
6	clock radio	24	10	240	0.24	$0.03
7	stereo	4	15	60	0.06	$0.01
8	computer	3	80	240	0.24	$0.03
9	dishwasher	1	1500	1500	1.5	$0.21
10	washing machine	1	450	450	0.45	$0.06
11	dryer	1	250	250	0.25	$0.04
12	Total	83	2942	9808	9.808	$1.37
13						

Figure 7. Completed electrical use spreadsheet in *AppleWorks* (*ClarisWorks*)

This concludes the activity.

Lab #10 *(cont.)*

AppleWorks (*ClarisWorks*) Template for Lab #10

	A	B	C	D	E	F
1	Appliance	Hours/Day Used	Wattage	Watt Hours	Kilowatt Hours	Cost
2	TV 19 inch color	5	60			
3	refrigerator	12	490			
4	incandescent light	8	75			
5	electric clock	24	12			
6	clock radio	24	10			
7	stereo	4	15			
8	computer	3	80			
9	dishwasher	1	1500			
10	washing machine	1	450			
11	dryer	1	250			
12	Total	83	2942			

Lab #10 *(cont.)*

Microsoft Excel Section

Procedure:

1. Begin this activity by explaining to your students that spreadsheet applications are not only used for creating charts and graphs but are also used like calculators to manipulate numerical data. Cells in a spreadsheet can be programmed to automatically perform mathematical calculations. This is how many businesses track inventory and sales. Explain to your class that they are going to create spreadsheets that track electrical use in a typical house.

2. Instruct your students to open new spreadsheet documents. Direct them to click in cell A1. To begin this exercise, they should create column labels for each type of data (*electrical use*) they are going to track. The label to be entered in cell A1 is (*Appliance*). After typing this label, students should press the **Tab** key on their keyboards to move to cell B1. The next label should read (*hours/day used*). The label for cell C1 should be (*wattage*), and the label for D1 should be (*watt-hours*). The label in cell E1 should be (*kilowatt-hours*), and the last label, located in cell F1, should be (*cost*). Remind students to press the **Tab** key after each entry. Once your students have entered all of their column labels, instruct them to change the font style to bold for each label and center the data in the cell. Your students' spreadsheets should now resemble Figure 8.

	A	B	C	D	E	F
1	Appliance	Hours/Day Used	Wattage	Watt Hours	Kilowatt Hours	Cost
2						
3						
4						
5						

Figure 8. Electrical use spreadsheet column labels

3. The appliances listed in the data sheet for this lab can be found in a typical house. Distribute a copy of the data sheet to each student. Instruct them to enter the appliances into the cells in column A, beginning with cell A2 and ending with cell A11.

4. Table 2 contains the average daily use in hours for each appliance. Instruct your class to enter the information into their spreadsheet and into the appropriate cell in column B.

Lab #10 *(cont.)*

5. Your students are now ready to enter from the data sheet the amount of wattage that these appliances consume when they are drawing power. Instruct your students to fill the required wattage into the correct cells in column C. When your class has entered all of their wattage requirements, their spreadsheets should resemble the one in Figure 9.

	A	B	C	D	E	F
1	Appliance	Hours/Day Used	Wattage	Watt Hours	Kilowatt Hours	Cost
2	TV 19 inch color	5	60			
3	refrigerator	12	490			
4	incandescent light	8	75			
5	electric clock	24	12			
6	clock radio	24	10			
7	stereo	4	15			
8	computer	3	80			
9	dishwasher	1	1500			
10	washing machine	1	450			
11	dryer	1	250			
12						

Figure 9. Completed hours/day used, and wattage requirements for the electrical use spreadsheet

6. Explain to your students that the next column of information, **Watt Hours**, is the manner in which the electric company measures electrical use. It is calculated by multiplying the wattage an appliance consumes by the hours a day it is being used. For example, if a sixty-watt light bulb were used for two hours, then its total consumption would be 120 watt-hours. Explain to them that they are going to enter in cell D2 a formula that will automatically calculate watt-hours. A cell formula is a mathematical expression that uses data from other cells to calculate. Explain to your class that they are going to create a cell formula that will multiply the number of hours a refrigerator is used by its wattage requirement.

Lab #10 *(cont.)*

7. Instruct students to click in cell D2 and type the formula (*=B2*C2*). Explain to your class that all cell formulas begin with the "=" sign. This tells the spreadsheet that a formula is being programmed into a cell. Also point out that the formula uses cell addresses in the mathematical expression. The sign for multiplication in a spreadsheet is the "*" symbol, or asterisk. Once they have entered the formula into the cell, they should press the **Return** key on their keyboards. Cell D2 displays the product of the data in cell B2 multiplied by the data in cell C2—300 watt-hours. Explain to your class that the contents of cell D2 will automatically change if the numbers in cells B2 or C2 are changed. For example, have your students change the number of hours the television is used from five to ten and press the **Return** key. Students should notice how the number in the watt-hours column also changed. This is one of the advantages for using spreadsheet formulas. You can constantly change the numbers in specific cells, and the formulas will still be applied. This is how businesses use spreadsheets to track inventory or automatically apply sales tax.

8. Now ask your students what they think the formula to automatically calculate watt-hours for the refrigerator should be. Instruct them to enter the formula (*=B3*C3*) into cell D3. Once they grasp the watt-hour formula concept, instruct them to complete the formulas for the rest of column D. When they are finished, their spreadsheets should resemble the one in Figure 10.

	D11	▼	=	=B11*C11		
						Workbo
	A	B	C	D	E	F
1	**Appliance**	**Hours/Day Used**	**Wattage**	**Watt Hours**	**Kilowatt Hours**	**Cost**
2	TV 19 inch color	5	60	300		
3	refrigerator	12	490	5880		
4	incandescent light	8	75	600		
5	electric clock	24	12	288		
6	clock radio	24	10	240		
7	stereo	4	15	60		
8	computer	3	80	240		
9	dishwasher	1	1500	1500		
10	washing machine	1	450	450		
11	dryer	1	250	250		
12						

Figure 10. Watt-hours automatically calculated by cell formulas in column D

Lab #10 *(cont.)*

9. Next, instruct your students to enter formulas into column E that will automatically calculate kilowatt-hours. Ask your students if they know what a kilowatt-hour is. (A kilowatt-hour equals one thousand watt-hours, and is used by the electric companies to measure electrical usage.) Electricity is consumed at such a high rate that watt-hours are too small of a measurement, so kilowatt-hour units are used instead. To calculate the kilowatt-hours used by the TV in one day, ask students what the formula should be in cell E2. Explain that they must divide the total amount of watts, which is displayed in cell D2, by one thousand (=D2/1000). Also point out that the symbol for division used in a spreadsheet formula is the "/" symbol, or backslash. They should enter the formula into cell D2 and press the **Return** key. The answer displayed in cell E2 of their spreadsheets should be (0.3). Once your students understand the kilowatt-hour formula, they should enter the rest of the formulas for column E. When they have completed this task, their spreadsheets should resemble the one in Figure 11.

	E11	▼	=	=D11/1000		
						lab10
	A	B	C	D	E	F
1	Appliance	Hours/Day Used	Wattage	Watt Hours	Kilowatt Hours	Cost
2	TV 19 inch color	5	60	300	0.3	
3	refrigerator	12	490	5880	5.88	
4	incandescent light	8	75	600	0.6	
5	electric clock	24	12	288	0.288	
6	clock radio	24	10	240	0.24	
7	stereo	4	15	60	0.06	
8	computer	3	80	240	0.24	
9	dishwasher	1	1500	1500	1.5	
10	washing machine	1	450	450	0.45	
11	dryer	1	250	250	0.25	
12						

Figure 11. Completed formulas for kilowatt-hours in column E

10. The final column of the electrical use spreadsheet deals with the cost of electricity. Explain to your students that the electric company uses the kilowatt-hour to calculate the cost of electricity. Although electrical costs vary by state and time of day, your students should use fourteen cents as the cost of a kilowatt-hour for this example. Ask your class what the formula should be in cell F2, where the cost of the electricity used by the TV is calculated. The answer is (=E2*.14). The answer in cell F2 should be (.042). This should be altered to show the value to the nearest cent. To accomplish this, your class should click in cell F2, then choose the **FORMAT** menu, and select *Cells*. Then your class should choose the **Number** tab, select **Currency** from the **Category** list, and click **OK**. The number in cell F2 should now be displayed in dollars and cents. Instruct your students to complete the cost formulas for the rest of column F. Remind them that they must also display all of the values in that column as currency.

Lab #10 *(cont.)*

11. Once your students have finished entering all of the formulas and formatting the last column, explain to them that *Microsoft Excel* provides many preprogrammed formulas. Students should click into cell A12, type the label (*Total*), and make it bold. In cell B12 they will use a preprogrammed formula that to all of the data in column B. To accomplish this, your class should choose the **INSERT** menu and select *Function*. The **Paste Function** window, which contains the preprogrammed functions, will now appear. Instruct your students to select **All** from the **Function** category list and scroll down the Function name list until they see the SUM function. Have them select this function, and click **OK**. The SUM window should appear and show cells B2 through B11 as selected. Ssee Figure 12.) If this is correct, instruct your students to click **OK**. The answer displayed in cell B12 should be (*83*).

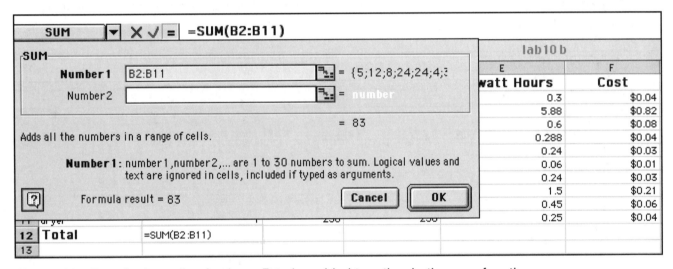

Figure 12. Data in the cells of column B to be added together in the sum function

Lab #10 *(cont.)*

12. Once your students have mastered the **Paste Function** command, instruct them to complete their spreadsheets by inserting and programming the sum function below each column. The next time they select *Function* from the **INSERT** menu, they can choose **Most Recently Used** from the **Function** category list. This will save them time when choosing the SUM function. Then they should change the format of the number in cell F12 to currency, and their spreadsheets should resemble the one in Figure 13. Have them save their files as (*elecuse*).

	F12 ▼ = =SUM(F2:F11)					
					lab10 b	
	A	B	C	D	E	F
1	**Appliance**	**Hours/Day Used**	**Wattage**	**Watt Hours**	**Kilowatt Hours**	**Cost**
2	TV 19 inch color	5	60	300	0.3	$0.04
3	refrigerator	12	490	5880	5.88	$0.82
4	incandescent light	8	75	600	0.6	$0.08
5	electric clock	24	12	288	0.288	$0.04
6	clock radio	24	10	240	0.24	$0.03
7	stereo	4	15	60	0.06	$0.01
8	computer	3	80	240	0.24	$0.03
9	dishwasher	1	1500	1500	1.5	$0.21
10	washing machine	1	450	450	0.45	$0.06
11	dryer	1	250	250	0.25	$0.04
12	**Total**	83	2942	9808	9.808	$1.37
13						

Figure 13. Completed electrical use spreadsheet in *Microsoft Excel*

This completes the activity.

Lab #10 *(cont.)*

Microsoft Excel Template for Lab #10

	A	B	C	D	E	F
1	**Appliance**	**Hours/Day Used**	**Wattage**	**Watt Hours**	**Kilowatt Hours**	**Cost**
2	TV 19 inch Color	5	60			
3	Refrigerator	12	490			
4	Incandescent Light	8	75			
5	Electric Clock	24	12			
6	Clock Radio	24	10			
7	Stereo	4	15			
8	Computer	3	80			
9	Dishwasher	1	1500			
10	Washing Machine	1	450			
11	Dryer	1	250			
12	**Total**	83	2942			

120

Lab #11 Advanced Spreadsheets: Unit Conversion Calculator

Note: Because of the differences that exist in creating a spreadsheet in *AppleWorks* (*ClarisWorks*) and *Microsoft Excel*, this lesson is divided into two separate sections. The first section deals with using *AppleWorks* (*ClarisWorks*), and the second section, beginning on page 128, focuses on *Microsoft Excel*.

Purpose:

Students program cells with the correct conversion formulas to create a metric/English unit conversion calculator.

Learning Objectives:

At the end of this lesson, each student will be able to:

- format a spreadsheet to act as a unit conversion calculator.

- create spreadsheet formulas within a cell.

- use cell formulas to convert the following English units to their metric equivalent: miles, feet, inches, acres, liquid ounces, quarts, gallons, dry ounces, pounds, tons, and Fahrenheit temperature.

- use cell formulas to calculate the following metric units to their English equivalent: kilometers, meters, centimeters, hectares, cubic centimeters, liters, grams, kilograms, Celsius temperature.

- utilize their spreadsheet unit conversion calculator to correctly convert assigned values for specific units of measurement.

Materials:

- *AppleWorks* (*ClarisWorks*) or *Microsoft Excel* spreadsheet application

- Conversion Factors hand out from page 122

- (*unitconv.cws*) *AppleWorks* (*ClarisWorks*) template or (*unitconv.xls*) *Microsoft Excel* template from the CD-ROM (optional)

  (If using the template, begin the lesson with step 3.)

Lab #11 *(cont.)*

Conversion Factors Hand Out

miles * 1.6 = kilometers	kilometers / 1.6 = miles
feet * 0.3 = meters	meters / 0.3 = feet
inches * 2.5 = centimeters	centimeters / 2.5 = inches
acres * 4.05 = hectares	hectares / 4.05 = acres
liquid ounces * 29.6 = cubic centimeters	cubic centimeter / 29.6 = liquid ounces
quarts * 0.946 = liters	liters / 0.946 = quarts
gallons * 3.79 = liters	liters / 3.79 = gallons
dry ounces * 28.35 = grams	grams / 28.35 = dry ounces
pounds * 453.6 = grams	grams / 453.6 = pounds
pounds * 0.453 = kilograms	kilograms / 0.453 = pounds
tons * 907.19 = kilograms	kilograms / 907.19 = tons
Fahrenheit = (F-32) / 1.8= Celsius	Celsius = (C*1.8) + 32 = Fahrenheit

Lab #11 *(cont.)*

AppleWorks (ClarisWorks) Section

Procedure:

1. Begin this activity by explaining to your students that spreadsheet applications are not only used for creating charts and graphs but also used like calculators to manipulate numerical data. Cells in a spreadsheet can be programmed to automatically perform mathematical calculations. This is how many businesses track inventory and sales. Explain to your class that Americans are unique in the world because they use two types of measurement, the English and the metric system. Sometimes it can be confusing to try to relate one system of measurement to the other. Explain to them that they will utilize spreadsheet formulas to create a unit conversion calculator that will make it easy for them to convert values between the English system and the metric system.

2. Direct your students to open new spreadsheet documents in *AppleWorks* (*ClarisWorks*). Then they should click in cell A1. They will need to create column labels for each unit of measurement that they are going to convert. The label, entered into cell A1, should be (*Value*). This is the column in which the specific value for a unit should be entered (*inches, miles, etc.*). Instruct them to press the **Tab** key on their keyboards to move them to cell B1. The next label should read (*Unit*). This column will list the specific units to be converted. The label for cell C1 is (*Equals*). This is just a filler label showing that the previous unit will be converted to the unit measurement of the following column. The label for D1 should be (*Value*). The value of the newly converted unit will be displayed in this column. The label for cell E1 should be (*Unit*). This column will show the converted unit of measurement. Once your students have entered all of their column labels, they should make the font style for each label bold and center the data in the cell. Your students' spreadsheets should now resemble the one in Figure 1.

A1	▼ *fx* ✕ ✓	Value		
	A	**B**	**C**	**D**	**E**
1	**Value**	**Unit**	**Equals**	**Value**	**Unit**
2					
3					
4					
5					

Figure 1. Unit conversion spreadsheet column labels

Lab #11 *(cont.)*

3. Next, explain to your students that the first formula they should program in their spreadsheets will be to convert miles to kilometers. They should first click into cell A2 and enter a (*1*). Then they should press the **Tab** key on the keyboard to move into cell B2. Here they should type the unit name (*miles*). Now, they should move into cell C2 and type (*equals*). They should skip cell D2 and move directly into cell E2. Ask your class what they think should be entered into this cell. The answer is (*kilometers*), the metric equivalent to miles.

4. Your class should now be ready to enter into cell D2 the formula that will convert the English value of miles into the metric equivalent of kilometers. Your class should click in cell D2 and then consult their Conversion Factors handout to find what the mathematical formula is for converting miles to kilometers (one mile is equal to 1.6 kilometers). Ask them what formula they should enter into cell D2 to automatically calculate the value entered in cell A2 to kilometers. Remind your students that all spreadsheet formulas must begin with the "=" sign, and the "*" symbol, or asterisk, is the sign used for multiplication. The answer should be (*=A2*1.6*). Once your class has typed this formula into cell D2, instruct them to press the **Return** key on their keyboards. The answer displayed in cell D2 should be (*1.6*). Their spreadsheets should now resemble the one in Figure 2.

D2	▼ *fx* ✕ ✓	=A2*1.6		
	A	**B**	**C**	**D**	**E**
1	Value	Unit	Equals	Value	Unit
2	1	miles	equals	1.60	kilometers
3					
4					
5					

Figure 2. First completed row for converting miles to kilometers

5. Once your students have successfully converted miles to kilometers, ask them to click in cell A2 once again. Inform them that they can enter any number of miles they want to convert to kilometers into cell A2, and the conversion will automatically appear in cell D2. Have students enter (*55*) into cell A2. The answer (*88*) will appear in cell D2.

6. Now instruct your class to click into cell B13 and type the unit (*Fahrenheit*). They should then move into cell C13 and enter the label (*equals*). Next, they should click in cell E13, where they should type the unit (*Celsius*). Explain to your students that because this conversion formula is somewhat more complex then the other conversion factors, you will go through this conversion together.

       124

Lab #11 *(cont.)*

7. Ask students to look at their handouts for the Fahrenheit to Celsius conversion formula. In this conversion, there is more than one calculation to perform. Ask your class if they know what the significance is of the parenthesis in the formula. (The parenthesis signifies that those calculations within must be performed first.) Instruct your students to click in cell D13 and enter the following formula: (*=(A13-32)/1.8*).

8. Next, instruct your students to click in cell A13 and type (*32*). The metric equivalent of 32 degrees Fahrenheit is zero degrees Celsius, so cell D13 should read (*0*). Once they have correctly entered and tested this formula, they should go back to row three and continue to enter the conversion formula for each unit. They should enter a (*1*) for the value of each unit in column A. This will make it easier to check their math, and assure them that the formula is calculating correctly.

9. When students have completed all of the unit conversions, they should highlight all of the numbers in column D, choose the **FORMAT** menu, and select *Number*. In the **Format Number, Date, and Time** window, they should select **Fixed**, and change the Precision box to (*2*). This should change the numbers to display only two decimal points. Once students have made this change, they should click the **OK** button. Your students' spreadsheets should now resemble the one in Figure 3.

10. To complete this activity, students should save their spreadsheets as (*unitcalc*), and use their unit conversion calculator to convert the following units: 5,280 feet, 12 inches, 8 liquid ounces, 4 quarts, 2000 pounds, and -40 degrees F. You or your students may wish to add more conversions if time allows.

This completes the activity.

Lab #11 (cont.)

Unit Conversion Spreadsheet

	A	B	C	D	E	F
1	Value	Unit	Equals	Value	Unit	
2	55	miles	Equals	88.00	kilometers	
3	1	feet	Equals	0.30	meters	
4	1	inches	Equals	2.50	centimeters	
5	1	acres	Equals	4.05	hectares	
6	1	liquid ounces	Equals	29.60	cubic centimeters	
7	1	quarts	Equals	0.95	liters	
8	1	gallons	Equals	3.79	liters	
9	1	dry ounces	Equals	28.35	grams	
10	1	pounds	Equals	453.60	grams	
11	1	pounds	Equals	0.45	kilograms	
12	1	tons	Equals	907.19	kilograms	
13	32	Fahrenheit	Equals	0.00	Celsius	
14	1	kilometers	Equals	0.62	miles	
15	1	meters	Equals	3.33	feet	
16	1	centimeters	Equals	0.40	inches	
17	1	hectares	Equals	0.25	acres	
18	1	cubic centimeters	Equals	0.03	liquid ounces	
19	1	liters	Equals	1.06	quarts	
20	1	liters	Equals	0.26	gallons	
21	1	grams	Equals	0.04	dry ounces	
22	1	grams	Equals	0.00	pounds	
23	1	kilograms	Equals	2.21	pounds	
24	1	kilograms	Equals	0.00	tons	
25	0	Celsius	Equals	32.00	Fahrenheit	
26						

Figure 3. Completed unit conversion calculator spreadsheet in *AppleWorks* (*ClarisWorks*)

Lab #11 *(cont.)*

AppleWorks (*ClarisWorks*) Template for Lab #11

	A	B	C	D	E
1	Value	Unit	Equals	Value	Unit
2	1	miles	Equals		
3	1	feet	Equals		
4	1	inches	Equals		
5	1	acres	Equals		
6	1	liquid ounces	Equals		
7	1	quarts	Equals		
8	1	gallons	Equals		
9	1	dry ounces	Equals		
10	1	pounds	Equals		
11	1	pounds	Equals		
12	1	tons	Equals		
13	32	Fahrenheit	Equals		
14	1	kilometers	Equals		
15	1	meters	Equals		
16	1	centimeters	Equals		
17	1	hectares	Equals		
18	1	cubic centimeters	Equals		
19	1	liters	Equals		
20	1	liters	Equals		
21	1	grams	Equals		
22	1	grams	Equals		
23	1	kilograms	Equals		
24	1	kilograms	Equals		
25	0	Celsius	Equals		

Lab #11 *(cont.)*

Microsoft Excel Section

1. Begin this activity by explaining to your students that spreadsheet applications are not only used for creating charts and graphs but also used like calculators to manipulate numerical data. Cells in a spreadsheet can be programmed to automatically perform mathematical calculations. This is how many businesses track inventory and sales. Explain to your class that Americans are unique in the world because they use two types of measurement, the English and the metric system. Sometimes it can be confusing to try to relate one system of measurement to the other. Explain to them that they will utilize spreadsheet formulas to create a unit conversion calculator that will make it easy for them to convert values between the English system and the metric system.

2. Direct your students to open new workbook documents in *Microsoft Excel*. Then they should click in cell A1. They should begin this exercise by creating column labels for each unit of measurement they will convert. The first label, entered into cell A1, should be (*Value*). This is the column in which the value of a unit to be converted will be entered. Once they have entered this label, instruct students to press the **Tab** key on their keyboards to move them to cell B1. The label for cell B1 should be (*Unit*). This column will show the specific unit to be converted (*inches, miles, etc.*). The label for cell C1 is (*Equals*). This is just a filler label showing that the previous unit will be converted to the unit measurement of the following column. The label for cell D1 should be (*Value*). The newly converted value will be displayed in this column. The label to be placed into cell E1 is (*Unit*). This column will show the converted unit of measurement. Once your students have entered all of their column labels, they should make the font style for each label bold and center the data in the cell. Your students' spreadsheets should now resemble the one in Figure 4.

	A	B	C	D	E
1	**Value**	**Unit**	**Equals**	**Value**	**Unit**
2					
3					
4					
5					

Figure 4. Unit conversion spreadsheet column labels

Lab #11 *(cont.)*

3. Next, explain to your students that the first formula they should program in their spreadsheets will be to convert miles to kilometers. First, they should click in cell A2 and enter a (*1*). Next, they should press the **Tab** key on their keyboards to move them to cell B2. Here they should type the unit name (*miles*). Now, they should move into cell C2 and type (*equals*). They should skip cell D2 and move directly into cell E2. Ask your class what they think should be entered into this cell. The answer is (*kilometers*), the metric equivalent to miles.

4. Your class should now be ready to enter into cell D2 the formula that will convert the English value of miles into the metric equivalent of kilometers. Your class should click in cell D2 and then consult their handouts to find the mathematical formula for converting miles to kilometers (one mile equals 1.6 kilometers). Ask them which formula they should enter into cell D2 to automatically calculate the value entered in cell A2 to kilometers. Remind your students that all spreadsheet formulas must begin with the "=" sign, and the "*" symbol, or asterisk, is the sign used for multiplication. The answer should be (*=A2*1.6*). Once your class has typed this formula into cell D2, instruct them to press the **Return** key on their keyboards. The answer displayed in cell D2 should be (*1.6*). Their spreadsheets should now resemble the one in Figure 5.

D2	▼	=	=A2*1.6	
				unitcalc
	A	B	C	D	E
1	**Value**	**Unit**	**Equals**	**Value**	**Unit**
2	1	miles	equals	1.6	kilometers
3					
4					
5					

Figure 5. First completed row for converting miles to kilometers

5. Once your students have successfully converted miles to kilometers, ask them to click in cell A2 once again. Inform them that they can enter into cell A2 any number of miles they want to convert to kilometers, and the conversion will automatically appear in cell D2. Have students enter (*55*) into cell A2. The value of cell D2 should automatically change to (*88*).

6. Now instruct your class to click into cell B13 and type the unit (*Fahrenheit*). They should then move into cell C13 and type (*equals*). Next, they should click into cell E13 where they should type the unit (*Celsius*). Explain to your students that because this conversion formula is somewhat more complex than the other conversion factors, you will go through this conversion together.

Lab #11 *(cont.)*

7. Ask students to look at their handout for the Fahrenheit to Celsius conversion formula. In this conversion there is more than one calculation to perform. Ask your class to explain the significance of the parenthesis in the formula. (The parenthesis signifies that those calculations within must be performed first.) Instruct your students to click into cell D13 and enter the following formula: (=(A13-32)/1.8).

8. Next, instruct your students to click into cell A13 and enter (*32*). The metric equivalent of 32 degrees Fahrenheit is zero degrees Celsius, so cell D13 should read (*0*). Once they have correctly entered and tested the formula, they should go back to row three and continue to enter the conversion formula for each unit. They should enter a (*1*) for the value of each unit in column A. This should make it easier to check their math, and assure them that the formula is calculating correctly.

9. When students have completed all of the unit conversions, they should highlight all of the numbers in column D, choose the **FORMAT** menu, and select *Number*. In the **Format Number, Date, and Time** window, they should select **Fixed**, and change the **Precision** box to (*2*). This should change the numbers to display only two decimal points. Once students have made this change, they should click the **OK** button. Your students' spreadsheets should now resemble the one in Figure 6.

10. To complete this activity, students should save their spreadsheets as (*unitcalc*) and use their unit conversion calculator to convert the following units: 5,280 feet, 12 inches, 8 liquid ounces, 4 quarts, 2000 pounds, and -40 degrees F. You or your students may wish to add more conversions if time allows.

This completes the activity.

Lab #11 *(cont.)*

	A	B	C	D	E
1	Value	Unit	Equals	Value	Unit
2	1	miles	Equals	1.60	kilometers
3	1	feet	Equals	0.30	meters
4	1	inches	Equals	2.50	centimeters
5	1	acres	Equals	4.05	hectares
6	1	liquid ounces	Equals	29.60	cubic centimeters
7	1	quarts	Equals	0.95	liters
8	1	gallons	Equals	3.79	liters
9	1	dry ounces	Equals	28.35	grams
10	1	pounds	Equals	453.60	grams
11	1	pounds	Equals	0.45	kilograms
12	1	tons	Equals	907.19	kilograms
13	32	Fahrenheit	Equals	0.00	Celsius
14	1	kilometers	Equals	0.63	miles
15	1	meters	Equals	3.33	feet
16	1	centimeters	Equals	0.40	inches
17	1	hectares	Equals	0.25	acres
18	1	cubic centimeters	Equals	0.03	liquid ounces
19	1	liters	Equals	1.06	quarts
20	1	liters	Equals	0.26	gallons
21	1	grams	Equals	0.04	dry ounces
22	1	grams	Equals	0.00	pounds
23	1	kilograms	Equals	2.21	pounds
24	1	kilograms	Equals	0.00	tons
25	0	Celsius	Equals	32.00	Fahrenheit
26					

Figure 6. Completed unit conversion calculator spreadsheet in *Microsoft Excel.*

Lab #11 *(cont.)*

Microsoft Excel Template for Lab #11

	A	B	C	D	E
1	**Value**	**Unit**	**Equals**	**Value**	**Unit**
2	1	miles	Equals		
3	1	feet	Equals		
4	1	inches	Equals		
5	1	acres	Equals		
6	1	liquid ounces	Equals		
7	1	quarts	Equals		
8	1	gallons	Equals		
9	1	dry ounces	Equals		
10	1	pounds	Equals		
11	1	pounds	Equals		
12	1	tons	Equals		
13	32	Fahrenheit	Equals		
14	1	kilometers	Equals		
15	1	meters	Equals		
16	1	centimeters	Equals		
17	1	hectares	Equals		
18	1	cubic centimeters	Equals		
19	1	liters	Equals		
20	1	liters	Equals		
21	1	grams	Equals		
22	1	grams	Equals		
23	1	kilograms	Equals		
24	1	kilograms	Equals		
25	0	Celsius	Equals		

Lab #12 Advanced Spreadsheets: Global Climate Change

Note: This lesson is divided into two sections. The first deals with using *AppleWorks* (*ClarisWorks*), and the second, beginning on page 140, focuses on *Microsoft Excel*.

Purpose:

Students utilize a spreadsheet to analyze data on atmospheric carbon dioxide concentration and change in global temperature. They use the data to generate a dual line chart that graphically displays the two sets of information.

Learning Objectives:

At the end of this lesson, each student will be able to:

- format a spreadsheet for efficient data entry.

- enter data into a spreadsheet.

- alter the style of a font in a spreadsheet cell.

- align data contained in spreadsheet cells.

- utilize the fill command to automatically enter data into specified cells.

- utilize selected cells in a spreadsheet to generate a dual line chart.

- create axis labels for a line chart.

- alter the appearance of data points on a line chart.

- create a title for a line chart.

- utilize a dual line chart to display the relationship between atmospheric carbon dioxide concentration and global temperature.

Materials:

- *AppleWorks* (*ClarisWorks*) or *Microsoft Excel* for Macintosh or Windows

- Data Sheet from page 134

- (*global.cws*) *AppleWorks* (*ClarisWorks*) template or (*global.xls*) *Microsoft Excel* template from the CD-ROM (optional)

   (If using the template file, begin the lesson with step 9.)

Lab #12 *(cont.)*

Data Sheet

Thousands of Years Ago	Carbon Dioxide	Change in Global Temperature
160	1.95	-9
150	2.05	-9.5
140	2.3	-7.5
130	2.95	-2
120	2.8	-2.5
110	2.7	-7
100	2.4	-4
90	2.4	-6.5
80	2.3	-5
70	2.4	-6.5
60	1.95	-7.7
50	2.18	-7.5
40	1.9	-7
30	2.2	-9
20	1.95	-10
10	2.55	-0.5
0	3.6	2.5

Lab #12 *(cont.)*

AppleWorks (ClarisWorks) Section

Procedure:

1. Introduce this activity by explaining to your students that they will use a spreadsheet to analyze data on atmospheric carbon dioxide concentration and global temperature. Scientists have long believed that there is a relationship between global temperature and atmospheric carbon dioxide. By studying gas bubbles trapped in glacial ice, researchers have created a record of global temperature change and atmospheric carbon dioxide concentration for the past 160,000 years. Explain to your students that they will take these records and analyze them to see if any relationship exists between carbon dioxide and global temperature. They will create colorful line charts to help them analyze the data.

2. Direct students to open a new spreadsheet document in *AppleWorks (ClarisWorks)*. They should click in cell A1 and type the label *(Thousands of Years Ago)*.

3. Next, they should press the **Tab** key on their keyboard, which will move them to cell B1. Instruct them to type the next label *(Carbon Dioxide)* in this cell. Have them press the **Tab** key once again to move them to cell C1 where they will type *(Change in Global Temperature)*.

4. Once they have entered the three labels, students should change the font style to bold, adjust the column width, and center all of the labels in each cell. Their spreadsheets should resemble the one in Figure 1.

	A	B	C
1	Thousands of Years Ago	Carbon Dioxide	Change in Global Temperature
2			
3			

Figure 1. Completed Global Climate Change column labels

5. Next, instruct your class that they should use the **Fill** command to automatically enter the numbers into the *(Thousands of Years Ago)* column. Explain to them that the **Fill Special** command is used to automatically enter into specified cells data like numbers, dates, months, and times.

6. Instruct your class to click into cell A2, hold their mouse buttons down, and drag down column A until they get to cell A18. They should then select the **CALCULATE** menu, and choose *Fill Special*. This will bring up the **Fill Special** window, where they should click the radio button next to **Number**. Next, they should click into the **Start** box and enter *(160)*. Then they should click into the **Increment By** box, and enter *(-10)*. They should then click the **OK** button. The selected cells of column A should have been automatically filled, beginning with 160 in cell A2 and ending with 1 in cell A18.

Lab #12 *(cont.)*

7. Now students can begin to enter from the data sheet the data for both carbon dioxide and change in global temperature for each year listed in their spreadsheets.

8. Once your students have finished entering their data, they should center all of the numbers in each cell, and their spreadsheets should resemble the one shown in Figure 2.

	A	B	C
1	**Thousands of Years Ago**	**Carbon Dioxide**	**Change in Global Temperature**
2	160	1.95	-9
3	150	2.05	-9.5
4	140	2.3	-7.5
5	130	2.95	-2
6	120	2.8	-2.5
7	110	2.7	-7
8	100	2.4	-4
9	90	2.4	-6.5
10	80	2.3	-5
11	70	2.4	-6.5
12	60	1.95	-7.7
13	50	2.18	-7.5
14	40	1.9	-7
15	30	2.2	-9
16	20	1.95	-10
17	10	2.55	-0.5
18	0	3.6	2.5
19			

Figure 2. Data entered into the carbon dioxide concentration and global temperature chart

Lab #12 *(cont.)*

9. Your class can now use the data they have just entered and formatted to create a line chart. Instruct your class to click in cell A1, hold down their mouse buttons, and drag over all of the cells that contain labels and data.

10. Once they have highlighted their data, instruct them to choose the **OPTIONS** menu and select *Make Chart*. This will bring up the **Chart Options** window, where they should select the **Line** chart.

11. Next, have them click the **Axes** button. Here they should click the **X-axis** radio button and enter (*Thousands of Years Ago*) into the **Axis label** box. They should then put a checkmark in the **Grid lines** box, and enter (*10*) in the **Step size** box.

12. Direct your students to click the **Series** button, click the arrow next to **All** in the **Edit Series** box, and select **Carbon Dioxide**. They should then change the **Display** as box to **Line**, and choose the **Symbol** that resembles a blue box. If the symbol choices are not blue, they should click the **Color** box and scroll to the blue color.

13. Now they should click the arrow next to **All** in the **Edit Series** box once again, and this time choose **Change in Global Temperature**. They should choose a triangle shape, and change the color to red by clicking the color box located next to **Symbol**.

14. Next, instruct your class to click the **Labels** button and enter (*Change in Atmospheric Temperature (C) and Carbon Dioxide Concentration (ppt)*) in the **Title** box. Explain to your students that the (*C*) represents degrees Celsius, and the (*ppt*) represents "parts per thousand." Then they should click the **General** button.

15. In the **General Section** window of the **Chart Options** window, your students should put a check mark in the box next to **First column** under the **Use numbers as labels in**. Your students should now click the **OK** button.

16. Explain to your students that they should adjust the size of their line chart in order to make it readable. To do this, they should choose the **WINDOW** or **VIEW** menu, depending on which version of *AppleWorks* (*ClarisWorks*) they are using, and select *Page View*. This should show the margins of the printable page.

17. Next, instruct your class to choose the **FILE** menu, and select *Page Setup*. They should then choose the **Landscape**, or sideways, orientation, and click the **OK** button. Finally, have your class click on the **100** button located in the lower left of their screen, and choose **67%**. This will reduce the view of their pages.

Lab #12 *(cont.)*

18. Now students should increase the size of their charts by clicking the anchor points located on each corner of the chart and dragging to the corners of the page within the margins. Their chart should now resemble the one in Figure 3. Ask your class if they can identify a relationship between atmospheric carbon dioxide and global temperature. What happens to the temperature when carbon dioxide concentration goes down? What happens to the temperature when carbon dioxide increases?

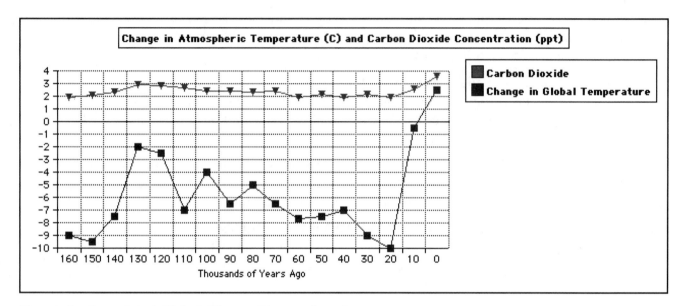

Figure 3. Completed Global Climate Change line chart

This completes the activity.

Lab #12 *(cont.)*

AppleWorks (*ClarisWorks*) Template for Lab #12

	A	B	C	D	E
1	Thousands of Years Ago	Carbon Dioxide	Change in Global Temperature		
2	160	1.95	-9		
3	150	2.05	-9.5		
4	140	2.3	-7.5		
5	130	2.95	-2		
6	120	2.8	-2.5		
7	110	2.7	-7		
8	100	2.4	-4		
9	90	2.4	-6.5		
10	80	2.3	-5		
11	70	2.4	-6.5		
12	60	1.95	-7.7		
13	50	2.18	-7.5		
14	40	1.9	-7		
15	30	2.2	-9		
16	20	1.95	-10		
17	10	2.55	-0.5		
18	0	3.6	2.5		

Lab #12 *(cont.)*

Microsoft Excel Section

1. Introduce this activity by explaining to your students that they will use a spreadsheet to analyze data on atmospheric carbon dioxide concentration and global temperature. Scientists have long believed that there is a relationship between global temperature and atmospheric carbon dioxide. By studying gas bubbles trapped in glacial ice, researchers have created a record of global temperature change and atmospheric carbon dioxide concentration for the past 160,000 years. Explain to your students that they will take these records and analyze them to see if any relationship exists between carbon dioxide and global temperature. They will create colorful line charts to help them analyze the data.

2. Begin this activity by having your students open a new workbook document in *Microsoft Excel*. Instruct them to click in cell A1 and type the label (*Thousands of Years Ago*).

3. Next, students should press the **Tab** key on their keyboards, which will move them to cell B1. In this cell, they should type the next label (*Carbon Dioxide*). Have them press the **Tab** key once again to move them into cell C1, where they will type (*Change in Global Temperature*).

4. Once they have entered all three of the labels, your class should change the font style to bold, adjust the column width, and center all of the labels in each cell. Their spreadsheets should resemble the one in Figure 4.

	A	B	C
1	**Thousands of Years Ago**	**Carbon Dioxide**	**Change in Global Temperature**
2			
3			
4			
5			

Figure 4. Completed Global Climate Change column labels

5. Next, instruct your class that they should use the **Fill** command to automatically enter the numbers into the (*Thousands of Years Ago*) column. Explain to them that the **Fill** command is used to automatically enter into specified cells data like numbers, dates, months, and times.

6. Instruct your class to click into cell A2, enter (160), and then press the **Return** or **Enter** key on their keyboards. Next, have them click into cell A2 once again. They should then go to the **EDIT** menu, select *Fill*, and then choose **Series**. This will bring up the **Series** window, where they should choose **Columns** under the **Series In** section. Under the **Type** section, they should select **Linear**. They should set the **Step Value to** (*-10*) and the **Stop Value to** (*0*). Finally, they should click the **OK** button. The selected cells of column A should have been automatically filled, beginning with 160 in cell A2 and ending with 1 in cell A18.

Lab #12 *(cont.)*

7. Now students can begin to enter from the data sheet the data for both carbon dioxide and change in global temperature for each year listed in their spreadsheets.

8. Once your students have finished entering their data, they should center all of the numbers in each cell, and their spreadsheets should resemble the one shown in Figure 5.

	A	B	C
1	**Thousands of Years Ago**	**Carbon Dioxide**	**Change in Global Temperature**
2	160	1.95	-9
3	150	2.05	-9.5
4	140	2.3	-7.5
5	130	2.95	-2
6	120	2.8	-2.5
7	110	2.7	-7
8	100	2.4	-4
9	90	2.4	-6.5
10	80	2.3	-5
11	70	2.4	-6.5
12	60	1.95	-7.7
13	50	2.18	-7.5
14	40	1.9	-7
15	30	2.2	-9
16	20	1.95	-10
17	10	2.55	-0.5
18	0	3.6	2.5
19			

Figure 5. Data entered into carbon dioxide concentration and global temperature columns

9. Next, instruct your students to use the **Chart Wizard** to make a chart from the data they have just entered into their spreadsheets. Have your students choose the **INSERT** menu, and select *Chart*. They can also select the **Chart Wizard** by clicking the **Chart Wizard** button on their toolbar.

10. Now they should choose **Line** from the **Chart Type** list, and select the **Line with markers displayed at each data value** chart from the **Chart sub-type** list. The first page of the **Chart Wizard** can be seen in Figure 6.

Lab #12 *(cont.)*

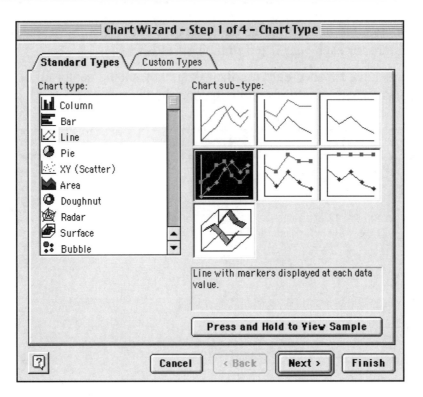

Figure 6. First page of the Chart Wizard

11. Instruct your students to click the **Next** button, and then click the **Series** tab. Next, they should click **Thousands of Years** in the **Series** list, and click the **Remove** button. Then, they should click the small red arrow icon located to the right of the **Category (X) axis labels** box. This should return your students to their spreadsheet, where they can click and drag over only the numbers in column A (not the Thousands of Years label). Once this is accomplished, they should click the **Next** button.

12. Next, your class should click the **Titles** tab, click into the **Chart title** box, and enter (*Change in Atmospheric Temperature (C) and Carbon Dioxide Concentration (ppt)*). Explain to your students that the "C" represents degrees Celsius, and the "ppt" represents "parts per thousand." In the **Category (X) axis** box, they should enter (*Thousands of Years Ago*). They can then click the **Next** button.

13. Finally, your class should choose how they want to display their charts in their documents. Instruct them to choose **As new sheet**, and title it (*Line Chart*). They should then click the **Finish** button to display their charts.

14. Your students' charts are now complete, and should resemble the one in Figure 7. Ask your class if they can identify a relationship between atmospheric carbon dioxide and global temperature. What happens to the temperature when carbon dioxide concentration goes down? What happens to the temperature when carbon dioxide increases?

This completes the activity.

Lab #12 *(cont.)*

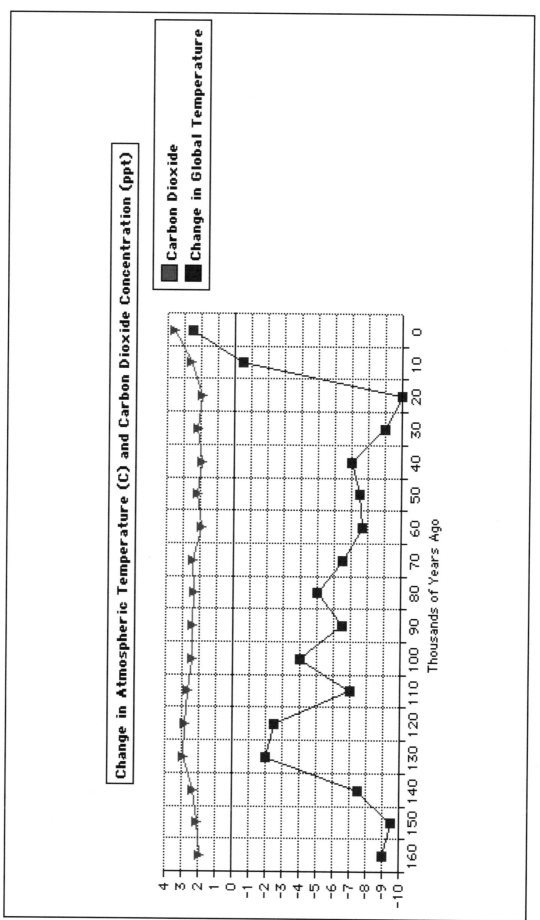

Figure 7. Completed Global Climate Change line chart

Lab #12 (cont.)

Microsoft Excel Template for Lab #12

	A	B	C	D
1	Thousands of Years Ago	Carbon Dioxide	Change in Global Temperature	
2	160	1.95	-9	
3	150	2.05	-9.5	
4	140	2.3	-7.5	
5	130	2.95	-2	
6	120	2.8	-2.5	
7	110	2.7	-7	
8	100	2.4	-4	
9	90	2.4	-6.5	
10	80	2.3	-5	
11	70	2.4	-6.5	
12	60	1.95	-7.7	
13	50	2.18	-7.5	
14	40	1.9	-7	
15	30	2.2	-9	
16	20	1.95	-10	
17	10	2.55	-0.5	
18	0	3.6	2.5	